INSTRUCTION WITHOUT BOUNDARIES

ENHANCE YOUR TEACHING STRATEGIES WITH TECHNOLOGY TOOLS IN ANY SETTING

MATTHEW RHOADS, ED.D.

JANELLE CLEVENGER MCLAUGHLIN, M.ED.

SHANNON MOORE, M.ED.

EduMatch
PUBLISHING

Published by EduMatch®
PO Box 150324, Alexandria, VA 22315
www.edumatchpublishing.com

ISBN: 978-1-953852-95-3

We dedicate this book to our families, friends, and mentors. Without you, we would not have been able to complete this project.

Additionally, we dedicate this book to all educators helping students navigate our ever-changing environments where boundaries and borders of our world transcend both physical and digital realms.

CONTENTS

INSTRUCTION WITHOUT BOUNDARIES

ENHANCE YOUR TEACHING STRATEGIES WITH TECHNOLOGY TOOLS IN ANY SETTING

Shifts and changes in life are inevitable, and even the slightest shift has the capacity to set an individual on either a positive or negative trajectory. Regardless of which path one is asked to navigate, disruption (both good and bad) is inevitable. When it comes to education, these inevitable disruptions can stifle or amplify student learning, and that is largely up to the educator; with the proper support and tools, educators everywhere will be able to roll with the punches and embrace all that lies ahead.

Imagine you are a student in today's classroom. As the school day begins, you know exactly what to expect because it has been the same routine since the beginning of your educational career—you sit quietly as the teacher lectures about the content of the day, you might fill out a worksheet or two, perhaps you take a quiz, or write an essay. It is the same routine day in and day out. And, while it is familiar and you have figured out how to "play the game of school" at least enough to get a decent score or grade, you have largely been accustomed to playing the role of "passive learner." Day in and day out, you let school happen to you. You may be a good student who gets your work done, but you often find yourself bored and desiring a bit more of a challenge once in a while.

Now imagine the same scenario, but instead of the teacher delivering the content, you are asked as a student to put on your investigative hat and dive deep into the content in an effort to think critically about it and how it fits into the world around you. Imagine you are engaged because your teachers are offering you choices, and you are given the opportunity to exemplify your learning in a way that makes sense to you—maybe it is a quiz or essay, but maybe it is also an opportunity to use your graphic, video, or audio design skills, maybe you finally get to show off your drawing skills, perhaps you get to participate in an engaging and collaborative discussion with peers. Imagine a classroom where those comfortable routines exist to keep you on track, but the activities, experiences, and strategies are constantly evolving. Instead of "letting school happen to you," you have become an active participant in the process, and you are able to embrace the creativity that lies within. Technology has become a tool that allows you to broaden your understanding and spread your wings as you dive into worlds previously unknown. As you navigate your educational career, a partnership has begun to form between you and your peers and you and your teacher.

Both scenarios are playing out in schools across America and throughout the world every single day. The reality is this… schools are evolving and changing and have been for quite a while. Truly, the last few years have been challenging and difficult to navigate, but fortunately, the recent experiences we have all endured as educators have sped up the changes that are taking place, and educators everywhere have risen to the challenge. It is time to embrace the evolution of education and this book is hopefully going to be the tool needed to spark creativity across the face of education in an effort to ensure students are given the opportunities they deserve.

Challenges of Instruction in Modern Day Classrooms

Educators everywhere consistently strive for growth and aim to evolve in their practice to ensure each student that enters their classroom has the opportunity to thrive. It has never become more clear than over the last few years that in order for educators to meet the needs of future-ready learners, they must adapt the ways in which they approach teaching and learning in their classrooms. In order to make the required shifts, it is essential that educators first name the challenges that exist in modern-day classrooms before they can brainstorm how to overcome said challenges. Here are the practices that must be re-evaluated if we want to prepare students for the future.

Moving Beyond Sit and Get

For many years, education has followed a "one size fits all" model, and that largely includes the element of lecture-style direct instruction. While direct instruction does have a place in education, it should not be the number one strategy an educator uses in their classroom. True direct instruction involves elements of lecture and moments where the students can converse and practice the material. Many classrooms, however, include lectures day in and day out where students passively receive the teacher-centered experience and are never given opportunities to dialogue/discuss or practice the implementation of the content. Sometimes they are even criticized or penalized when they do not get it just right.

Access and Equity

The last ten years have largely demonstrated that access to WiFi and technology is not equal across all school sites; in fact, this has become a growing concern over the last few years, and school districts have scrambled to get equipment in students' hands due to the toggle between traditional in-person schooling and virtual learning. It is a problem that has to be solved in an effort to give all students the chance to be successful in the ever-changing landscape that exists today. Future industries expect students to be technically savvy, and schools have an obligation to bridge the digital divide and ensure we are preparing future-ready students.

Additionally, equity is an issue in regards to the relevancy of the curriculum that exists in our schools today. Many Black, Indigenous, People of Color (BIPOC) or Lesbian, Gay, Bisexual, Transgender, Queer, Intersex (LGBTQ+) students are not seeing themselves represented in the curriculum and therefore struggle to make connections; this is an equity and access issue. If students cannot connect to the curriculum, then we are not providing them the opportunity to engage with the curriculum in a purposeful and meaningful way. It is essential that we are mindful of interests, passions, culture, attitudes, experiences, et cetera when planning lessons in the classroom; all students deserve a chance to see themselves in the content they are learning. Relevancy to the student matters as they move toward success.

Preparing Students for the Work World

Future-ready students will need to be resilient problem-solvers, negotiators, and critical thinkers. They will need to refrain from imposing judgment on others, and their emotional and social intelligence will need to be strong. Future jobs will require innovation and creativity. Future employers will want those that have strong time management skills and can effectively navigate challenging interpersonal situations. Effective employees will be quality communicators and understand the need for cognitive flexibility. Digital and data literacy and computational thinking will be valued in future careers. Classrooms today largely are driven by the content standards that dictate the skills necessary to be successful, but people skills, STEM skills, creative thinking skills, et cetera are all equally important. If students are not receiving opportunities to cultivate these skills, they will find themselves at a deficit once they graduate and enter the workforce where jobs are changing and evolving more so than ever before.

Environment/Space

As education shifts, the environment and space where learning takes place play an important role in the success of our learners. The last few years have only proven this as students have had to switch between traditional classrooms, to blended learning environments, to virtual online learning. Environment and space matter to the comfortability and security that students experience throughout their learning journey. Educators have to be mindful of this new reality of instruction without boundaries and must become equipped to maintain a traditional physical classroom learning environment and a digital space concurrently if we want students to remain resilient throughout their educational careers. If educators solely rely on traditional in-person methods of classroom routines and procedures, then students will be left behind and confused, neither of which is conducive to learning in our globally interconnected world.

Education is changing. Modern-day classrooms have to look different. As experience has shown, life will continue to throw curveballs at us, and without adapting and remaining flexible, we are bound to get beamed by one or two. Educators everywhere could lament the fact that "nothing is fair," or they can rise to the challenge, embrace the innovative thinking required to overcome these challenges, and join in as the face of education positively transforms before their eyes. So what is the new reality? What should educators be ready for?

The Classroom Without Instructional Boundaries

The world of education has been given a taste of what it means to remain flexible in educational spaces. The traditional four-wall classroom environment is no longer the only means with which students can learn; schools need to embrace the ever-changing face of education and realize that student learning isn't constricted or limited by spaces anymore. Pandemic education has made it evident that learning can happen within a traditional classroom, within a digital classroom, and within a combination of the two; if education is to evolve with the time, it is time to embrace the reality of a classroom without instructional boundaries. Eventually, the uncertainty of COVID education will shift, but a new uncertainty will take its place; that is just how the world works, so in an effort to embrace the new abnormal, educators need to be deliberate about how and where the content is being delivered. Educators need to adapt to the technological need required for such shifts, and while this will be a challenge for many, it is the future of education, and without the shift, students will not be given the greatest opportunity they can to be successful. Instruction without boundaries is here to stay, and this text will help educators navigate this new reality.

PURPOSE OF THE BOOK—HOW WE CAN HELP AMPLIFY STUDENT LEARNING ANYWHERE

The goal of any good educator is to ensure students are learning at their greatest capacity. This book will help maximize student learning by offering research-based instructional strategies that have been proven effective. Throughout this book, educators can hone in on specific areas of instructional design (i.e., collaboration, classroom routines, engagement) and, within those chapters, get suggestions for how to implement tried-and-true strategies that promote student learning. In addition, all of these strategies are paired with effective educational technology approaches that will encourage participation from all learners despite the environment. In essence, this text acts as a playbook that teachers can go to when they are attempting to mix up the strategies they use in the classroom in an effort to make students active participants in the learning process.

Provide Instruction in Any Classroom Setting

Each instructional strategy included in this book provides practical examples that show how you can seamlessly integrate the strategy in a traditional in-person classroom, a blended learning experience, or in a completely online setting. Recent history has shown that the educational experience is no longer confined to one space, but rather has the capacity to span a variety of environments, and therefore, the strategies and EdTech provided throughout will include concrete examples that meet that reality.

A FRAMEWORK TO THINK ABOUT WHILE INTEGRATING INSTRUCTIONAL STRATEGIES AND EDTECH

When integrating instructional strategies with EdTech in classrooms without boundaries, there are three considerations we want to discuss before we jump into the contents of this book. Each of these considerations can create a framework to help us integrate the strategies and EdTech together effectively without being overwhelmed. Together in tandem, we will discuss how being aware of cognitive load, instituting the SAMR Model, and having the "think less is more" mindset create the framework of strategy and EdTech integration that can go a long way in a classroom without instructional boundaries.

The Big Elephant in the Room—Cognitive Load

Cognitive load essentially means the amount of working memory that is used while information is being presented to a learner. Cognitive load is important to understand because we can only process so much information as a learner, which will then be transferred to our long-term memory by our working memory (Sweller, 1998). This is something we must be aware of as educators because learning new information requires a mental effort resulting in a load on our students' working memories. It affects learning outcomes because our working memory has only so much capacity to take on so much new information and tasks all at once (Leahy & Sweller, 2008). For example, the task complexity and the student's prior knowledge and experiences completing that task all help counteract the amount of cognitive load they may experience (Leahy & Sweller, 2008). Each of these facets must be taken into consideration for all decisions made in a classroom by a teacher.

Throughout the book, cognitive load will be brought up or alluded to because of its importance when integrating new strategies and EdTech integrations, as it directly affects student learning. Therefore, as discussed in a moment, the prevailing theme of **think less is more** is critical for all things we do in our classroom as well as how we take what we learn from this book to implement it into our instruction.

A Quick Thought About the SAMR Model

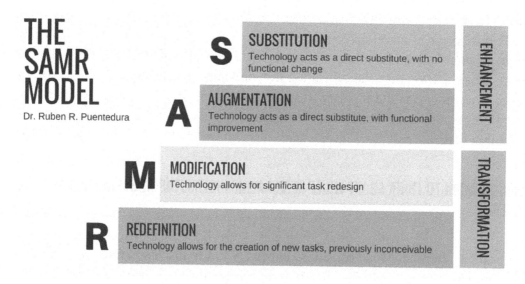

Lefflerd, CC BY-SA 4.0 <https://creativecommons.org/licenses/by-sa/4.0>, via Wikimedia Commons

The Substitution, Augmentation, Modification, and Redefinition Model (SAMR) model developed by Puentedura (2013) gives us a framework for how we can think about incorporating technology within our instruction. The goal of the SAMR model is to not only enhance the instruction taking place but also transform it. Most importantly, the SAMR model works in classrooms without boundaries because it provides a wide range of strategies to be incorporated into our instruction regardless of whether we are in an online, blended, or traditional classroom setting. Thus, our goal with this book is to transform how instruction takes place with the strategy and EdTech integration going hand in hand. As a result, throughout the book, the instructional integrations with EdTech tools will illustrate how this is done in modern classrooms.

Think Less is More Mindset

There are only so many new practices we can incorporate into our instructional toolboxes at a time. We want to explore and practice, but not overwhelm ourselves. Therefore, we want to focus on two to five strategies while learning their EdTech integrations by exploring, practicing, and determining whether we want them to be incorporated long-term into our instruction.

This is a mindset. While this book provides many instructional strategies and integrations, being strategic is key to being successful with the strategies provided. Taking the opportunity to see what may work best for you at a given time is key. You may want to focus on two to three strategies to add this semester and then see if you would like to add three strategies the following semester. However, we do not want you to find ten strategies and integrations and try to implement them all at once. This is too much for both you and your students. As a result, the best strategy is to read the book entirely and then come back time and time again when you want to review, implement, and add strategies and integrations to your practice.

We want to think less is more in order to focus on quality over quantity. This will create the time to explore, practice, and implement more effectively, which will benefit your students and you!

ORGANIZATION OF BOOK

This book is organized into six chapters. Each chapter helps not only build foundations for classrooms without instructional boundaries but also to enhance the learning of your students in new innovative ways. **Besides chapter one, the content does not progress linearly**. Rather, it expands out in a circular manner. As you move through the chapters, your instructional toolkit will expand. Additionally, many of the strategies and integrations discussed can be utilized in one or more areas. For example, a strategy like think, write, pair, and share can be discussed as an engagement and collaborative strategy. Therefore, as you learn more, think about how the strategies and integrations outlined in this book can be delivered in a multi-faceted manner. Lastly, we suggest coming back to chapters you have read in the future as we want you to have a "think less is more" thought process when you begin taking the strategies and integrations learned in this book to then begin implementing in your classroom.

Chapter 1: Classroom Routines Without Boundaries

Chapter One is an introduction of how to build foundational classroom routines to increase student learning within any classroom setting. This chapter highlights the importance of establishing routines in a traditional and digital classroom and is broken into six major categories to consider: student accessibility, social-emotional learning, flexibility and responsive environments, communication, leveraging technology, and navigating digital and physical spaces. Additionally, the chapter notes how to leverage a learning management system to ensure each learner, regardless of space, can effectively access the material.

Chapter 2: Student Engagement in Classrooms Without Defined Borders

Chapter Two provides a series of research-based instructional strategies which enhance student engagement and illustrate student learning within various classroom settings. An effective engagement framework, which includes four main approaches (building connections with students, intentional design, students as co-creators of knowledge, and gamified learning) is established in order to provide practical ideas as to how educators can cultivate classroom environments that foster student engagement.

Chapter 3: Student Collaboration within Classrooms that Transcend Boundaries

Chapter Three begins by defining student collaboration, then highlights how to optimize collaboration within any classroom setting, followed by outlining the benefits of collaboration related to student learning, and finishes with considerations to think about when implementing student collaboration strategies in any classroom setting. Within this chapter's vignettes, you will find six effective collaborative instructional strategies that enhance learning: concept making, think, pair, and share, jigsaw, Socratic seminar, structured academic controversy, and gallery walks.

Chapter 4: Inquiry and Critical Thinking Strategies Amplified by Technology

Chapter Four provides several frameworks that promote higher-order and critical thinking skills in the classroom. The Teaching and Learning Inquiry Framework (TLIF) by Molebash, Lee, and Heinecke (2019) is used to illustrate how the strategies, skills associated with critical thinking, common core standards, and universal design for learning framework can be synthesized together to propel our instruction to help spark inquiry and critical thinking.

Chapter 5: Creativity and Innovation Within Modern Classrooms Without Boundaries

Chapter Five is guided by the concepts outlined in the Partnership of 21st-century skills Framework, as well as insight provided by the Design Thinking and Diffusion of Innovation Theory, all of which provide pragmatic approaches to integrate creativity and innovation into the classroom. Eight instructional strategies that are derived from these conversations are illustrated: Design Thinking, Makerspace, Choice Boards, Genius Hour, Play and Prototyping, and Virtual Reality to Experience.

Chapter 6: The Age of Formative Assessment and Feedback

Chapter Six establishes a guided approach to implementing research-based strategies on assessment and feedback to increase student learning by strategically monitoring and adjusting instruction. The chapter outlines effective approaches to formative assessment, alternative assessments, and choice-based assessments in an effort to enhance student ownership over their learning.

——————

How to Use This Book

There are numerous ways to use this book. We will illustrate how it can be utilized as: a playbook, a medium to help you innovate and reflect, sharing and connecting with a Professional Learning Network (PLN), and a mechanism for professional development and learning. All of these areas will strengthen your teaching and instruction within classrooms without boundaries.

As a Playbook

This book truly is for any educator at every level. It was specifically designed to be used as a playbook, making it simpler to integrate research-based instructional strategies with common EdTech tools. The first chapter on digital classroom routines supports you in setting up your blended learning environment and sets the stage to move through the other chapters at your discretion. The design also integrates nicely with personal and professional goals you have set for yourself. If you notice that student engagement has been diminishing, start with the Engagement chapter. After reading through the chapter, choose one or two strategies to try first. Pick and choose the strategies that feel the most comfortable to you, to begin with. After you've experienced that initial success, then you can push yourself (and your students) into areas that are a bit less comfortable for greater growth. After you see engagement successes, move to another chapter of interest. The choice of order is completely up to you.

Innovate and Reflect

We also hope you use this book as your guide for innovation and reflection. The strategies in this book are not new, and that was intentional. We chose those that have been proven time and again and innovated in ways that incorporated EdTech for greater engagement, efficiency, and/or effectiveness in the classroom. These ideas are only a jumping-off point. Use the strategies and integrations as a springboard to your own iterations and innovations. The important part is to spend time reflecting after you try out something new to determine if it was the best choice of strategy and tool for that lesson and with those students. John Dewey said, "We do not learn from experience...we learn from reflecting on experience." It's through that reflection that true growth occurs for both teachers and students. Set aside regular time for intentional reflection as you put the strategies from this book into practice.

Share with Your PLN

We also know that sharing the learning process with others solidifies it more for us. A Professional Learning Network is one of the most powerful learning tools educators have at their fingertips. Your PLN brings perspectives other than your own, while also giving you people to reflect with, collaborate with, and learn from. Daniel Tobin first wrote about PLNs back in 1998. In an updated article, he said, "The members of your network should be people, both inside and outside of your work group and your company, who have the knowledge that you are trying to master and who are willing to share their knowledge and experience with you" (Tobin, 2017, p. 1). Whether the PLN is developed through Twitter, LinkedIn, Facebook, or with colleagues around your school and district, everyone learns more when we share what we are doing. If you find a strategy that is extremely effective, tell someone. If you learn a new EdTech tool that is more engaging, share it with others. We will also be sharing our learning and yours with our own PLN, and we always welcome the opportunity to add more friends to our circle. Use #**Instruct-WithoutBoundaries** when tweeting or sharing on Instagram. Check out our website, www.InstructWithoutBoundaries.com, to sign up for alerts regarding other opportunities to learn together, such as book clubs, interactive learning sessions, and more.

As a Mechanism for Professional Development and Learning

Books have long been much-loved conduits for continuous learning. This one also provides a mechanism for professional development. By linking your reading plan to a goal and setting aside time for intentional reflection, you are essentially building your own professional learning plan. By sharing what you are doing, trying, and learning with others, you are not only benefiting your own growth, but you are sharing that professional development with other educators. These are all fairly organic processes, but you can also choose to lead other learners through a more formal professional learning process by organizing a book study or sharing at a faculty meeting. The growth opportunities are endless and help you be that lead learner in your classroom and school while feeding your desire to continually hone your craft.

Moving Forward to a Classroom Without Instructional Boundaries

Moving forward, set your own path for this learning journey. Read in whatever order you want. Read a few pages or a few chapters at a time. Give yourself permission to try, fail, innovate, and try again. Not everything will work seamlessly the first time, but most of the time, it's worth a second chance. We all want to provide the best learning environments for our students, so dig in and enjoy the ride!

CHAPTER 1
CLASSROOM ROUTINES WITHOUT BOUNDARIES

Today's classroom experience involves walking into two realms: physical and digital. Due to the unavoidable onset of online learning and the ability of EdTech tools to be implemented within physical in-person and online digital settings, classroom environments tend to vacillate between multiple settings. Ultimately, this allows learning to take place inside and outside of school buildings; however, there are many implications regarding how this operates for teachers and students.

As educators navigate this toggle, questions arise as to how to develop classroom routines that span in-person and digital online settings. How do we set up classroom routines and norms to ensure students understand classroom expectations in both spheres? What are research-based strategies for in-person and digital routines that blend into both settings? How can we integrate EdTech tools into our routines and digital classroom spaces? How do we ensure we model classroom citizenship that encompasses both physical and digital realms? All of these questions are essential to consider as routines must be catered to include both spaces within modern classrooms. When these questions are answered, we can develop classroom routines that heighten our students' abilities to learn both in-person and in digital settings, as well as thrive as a citizen within a community of learners.

Routines are difficult and take time to implement and maintain. Additionally, they require constant modeling, structure, and daily repetition to make them a normal part of your classroom structure. Navigating and implementing these routines across in-person and digital settings adds an additional layer of complexity because the number of routines may increase, in addition to the fact that these routines will most likely take place within multiple settings. Navigating the LMS and integration of additional EdTech tools becomes a major consideration that routines must be built around. Teachers must be pragmatic in their approach to planning their routines; often, this might include student participation and feedback. Our goal is to simplify the process of developing and implementing routines for in-person and digital classroom spaces in addition to scenarios when both settings blend together. Throughout this chapter, we want you to focus on how we can integrate routines with EdTech to work within any education environment. As you read through the research and vignettes exemplifying how routines can be implemented in classrooms, try to remember "less is more" and evaluate how the routines are being spelled out. Reflect on whether or not they can be integrated into your classroom now or in the future. We are not asking you to reinvent the wheel of your classroom routines. We are asking you to determine whether these routines will make your life and the lives of your students easier and more efficient. Our secondary goal is to show you that they are efficient and effective, which we hope will result in the adoption of many of them over time into your classroom instruction and culture. In the same manner, you will have to sell the routines to your students and gradually build them over time into your instruction and classroom environments. Keep this in mind as well when thinking about selecting and implementing routines. Furthermore, as you progress through the chapter, the focus is on creating more efficient transitions and routines in your classroom. You will soon learn from the research that more learning will take place. Thus, by highlighting routines, student learning will be fostered as a result.

Before jumping into the research, we want to reiterate that teachers must be intentional in their routines and provide clear purposes and expectations for their students. Teacher clarity is essential for this to occur, which will be the foundation of the research discussed in this chapter. Much of the research then jumps to defining classroom routines, outlining which routines are the best ones to use, and then discussing how we can implement them within in-person and digital settings. After perusing this chapter, you will see that it provides a treasure trove of routines that span instructional settings as well as blends them together. As you know, digital and in-person spaces are the norm now in K-12 education. These types of routines will encompass both settings in a simultaneous fashion and are here to stay!

What are Classroom Routines?

Classroom routines allow students to be oriented to the activity or set of tasks teachers want them to complete. Classrooms that are structured yet flexible provide prime opportunities for students to learn. We have all seen classrooms that are disoriented and organized. Some of the best classrooms may look like controlled chaos. Other classrooms may look very structured in how they are run. Our goal is to discuss a two-faceted formula that helps teachers implement strong routines that put students in good positions to learn regardless of your classroom setting. Then, we will describe how classroom routines should be centered around building connection, climate, instruction, and curriculum.

In a two-fold approach, having solid classroom routines begins with teacher clarity as well as spending a good amount of time modeling and orienting students to a task or activity in a classroom (Cameron, Connor, Morrison, & Jewkes, 2008; Fisher, Fry, & Hattie, 2020). Teacher clarity means teaching is both organized and intentional in nature. It encompasses clear and concise directions, which allows our students to plan, predict, set goals, and be able to assess their own progress in class (Hattie, 2012). Moving parallel with teacher clarity is intentionality relating to modeling how routines should look within a classroom. Ultimately, the more time devoted to reinforcing routines and showing your students again and again what they look like minimizes transition time from activity to activity, which improves the flow of a lesson and maximizes student learning (Cameron et al., 2008).

Classroom routines fall under the three major categories: connections, climate, and instruction and curriculum. Connection is not the same connection in terms of relationship building. Rather, it is a deliberate contextualization of the classroom's content and skills in addition to providing a lens as to what is expected of the students (Reppeto, Cavanaugh, Water,& Liu, 2010). Teachers can provide context to their routines while at the same time providing step-by-step instructions to help students conceptualize where they are at in the present as well as where they will go in the future. Second, routines centered around climate are established by developing positive routines and learning opportunities that help cultivate a positive classroom culture. Establishing routines and norms centered around positive and restorative behaviors, openness, treating others the way they would like to be treated, discussion and dialogue, and student collaboration all help cultivate a positive classroom climate and experience for students and teachers (Repetto et al., 2010). Third, in regard to instruction and curriculum, routines should be focused on academic support, daily engagement strategies, and opportunities for active student participation and collaboration (Boat & Ricomini, 2006; Fisher et al., 2020; Repetto et al., 2010).

Overall, these routines are built into your instructional design and lesson plans that occur daily. For example, for active student engagement, a routine can be centered around an instructional strategy like a quick write that is integrated within interactive slides or a digital discussion board. Each day students should know how to access, actively participate and complete the task, and collaborate with their peers. Another example is an instructional routine centered around the LMS. Students have access to a series of screencast videos that show them how they can access the material, receive additional support, and navigate digital and in-person classroom activities.

Altogether, routines centered around connection, climate, and instruction and curriculum are all critical for providing your students the opportunity to learn the concepts and skills that are taught within your classroom. Focusing on implementing three to five major routines each within the categories of connection, climate, and instruction will be enough at any given time to foster a strong learning environment for your students within any classroom setting.

Classrooms Have Digitized—The LMS & Digital Routines

Classrooms have changed immensely. Now, classrooms have a major digital and online component that goes along with the in-person setting. Sometimes, the classroom is entirely digital. With this said, regardless of the classroom setting, most of the content that is delivered from a teacher to students is now digital in nature. While some of the content remains to be non-digital, any non-digital content can be uploaded to the Learning Management System (LMS). LMSs have become central to how classrooms have become digitized.

LMSs drive content delivery in today's classrooms. They serve as the main platform through which online and digital activities can be accessed. It is becoming the norm that entire classes can be stored and deployed through an LMS; they are essentially the hub that allows a teacher to store content, hyperlink other EdTech tools to be utilized by students, and deliver content to students.

When thinking about classroom routines in a digitized classroom, the LMS is central to that discussion as routines must be built around it for students to understand how they can navigate and how content is being delivered by a teacher. This is where teachers can create routines related to communication and feedback, time management during synchronous and asynchronous learning, sharing of links and applications, and walking through how to navigate the LMS and EdTech tools that are utilized on a daily basis (Darling-Hammond, 2012; Moore & Kearsley, 2011; Ng, 2007).

Beyond the LMS—A Synthesis of Digital and In-Person Routines

Beyond the LMS, there are a number of organizational routines and procedures to think about for your digital and in-person classroom settings. We must remember that each of these settings is now blended together. Therefore, when thinking about routines, we must think about how they may appear in both a digital and online setting, along with being in a physical and in-person setting. Our conversation will focus on setting up a weekly agenda, turning in assignments and accessing tasks, being intentional with our LMS, and EdTech tool use in our lesson design, and some recommendations on best practices to implement these routines within modern classroom settings.

First, let's discuss routines related to teacher clarity and giving your students an idea of what's going on in a classroom on a daily and weekly basis. Frontloading students with information regarding the week is a major source of establishing organizational cohesiveness in a classroom. Educators can provide students with a weekly agenda and then break it up daily. It is important to house it in viewable areas both online and in-person. This can be done on the LMS or a slidedeck so students can access the daily and weekly agenda.

Another aspect we must be aware of is turning in assignments and tasks. This routine is a procedure that is worked on from the beginning of the year until the end of the year, as it's critical for students to receive feedback from their teacher on the work they have accessed and used to provide evidence of learning. Digitally, there are routines for turning in work as evidence of student learning on the LMS. Additionally, there must also be routines for turning in physical paper assignments somewhere in the classroom as another mechanism to collect evidence of student learning. Therefore, when designing our classroom, we must develop routines for both of these instances in addition to returning student work with feedback.

To cultivate transitions from one task to the other, provide students with physical cues to respond with physical bodily movements (e.g., thumbs up and down, hand gestures, physical objects symbolizing an action [e.g., talking sticks, different colors of paper]) during synchronous learning sessions. To further facilitate transitions, we can use music throughout the lesson or school day during synchronous instruction to signify when it's time to move to a different activity. During asynchronous learning time, we can integrate asynchronous routines into a classroom by creating playlists that provide students opportunities and choice to practice skills taught during synchronous learning sessions.

When designing a classroom with digital norms and routines, teachers must be intentional about the design of how their LMS and EdTech tools are assembled and utilized by students. When designing a digital classroom environment, be sure to keep the LMS uniform throughout, organize work by weeks or units, keep the number of links limited, and ensure students only have to click the mouse or laptop directional pad, or tap the touchscreen three to four times to navigate the digital classroom environment. Educators should consider minimizing the number of clicks even further for lower elementary students. Furthermore, digital routines should be modeled, rehearsed, and repeated throughout the time in class (Fisher et al., 2020; Rhoads, 2021). Screencasts can be utilized within the LMS demonstrating various classroom routines that are digital and in-person for students to review. All of this is intentional and integrated into the design of your lesson.

To facilitate these routines, Packard (2013) recommends several suggestions to cultivate classroom routines and cultures for online and digital learning settings that also blend into in-person classroom settings. First, providing respect, grace, timely feedback, and monitoring student understanding of the expectations in online and in-person settings is essential to making classroom norms work effectively. Establish a positive classroom climate by easing your way into developing routines. Start simply and with a few checks for understanding, show grace and respect, and provide feedback as the routines are integrated into a classroom. Then, the second step of recommendations relates to providing opportunities for students to create content in both settings as well as share that content with the school community, frequent check-ins with students online and in-person, and provide a number of instructional communication strategies (e.g., text, phone, email, chat, and video) (Packard, 2013).

Best Practices for Digital Classroom Routines for ALL Classrooms According to the Research

Before diving into how we can facilitate classroom routines by integrating a number of strategies and design elements with EdTech tools into your lessons and classroom culture, let's summarize some best practices for facilitating classroom routines within digital and online settings that also blend into in-person classroom settings. Anthony (2019) outlined four effective strategies to help ensure teachers can implement routines in blended and online classrooms to help students navigate the various classroom and learning spaces. Before speaking specifically about an assortment of strategies that support these components, we will first discuss Anthony's (2019) four major components we need to think about as we develop and implement routines for blended and online classrooms.

1. Be flexible and responsive. Create variety and flexibility in routines that are engaging, which includes providing student roles.
2. Communicate with students through a variety of different means.
3. Leverage routines centered around technology.
4. Make sure the physical classroom and the LMS are organized, and routines are built around navigating each.

Strategies that make these components come to life include several direct actions teachers can implement into their instruction to help build routines. For example, the first consideration is centered around flexibility and responsiveness in developing routines for students. Teachers can adjust routines and instruction based on time allotments, student groupings, and places of learning (LEAP, 2017). Depending on the activity or transition within a lesson, teachers can adjust routines based on how much time they have. Some activities may take longer than others; for example, a quick write or warm-up may be shorter than an independent practice activity. The transition from the independent activity on a given day, however, may take longer as student grouping must take place. Similarly, breakout rooms are developed in online synchronous class sessions. Keep in mind that breakout room norms and routines may be different from physical in-person collaboration taking place at a table. Therefore, considerations, as discussed above, are important to note as routines will need to be developed for each of these examples.

Next, let's discuss how we can communicate routines to students. Teachers should be clear and direct about the lesson objectives and outcomes. Clearly written and verbal directions related to the routines and procedures of specific activities, and explicit instruction using modeling and think-alouds are key (Anthony, 2019; Hattie, 2009). Communication will look different in digital and in-person classroom environments. In both settings, we must have visuals of the lesson objectives and outcomes; although, in these different spaces, visuals vary. A classic slideshow can be shown in-person, but cannot be fully accessed at any time unless a student can access it through the LMS. In addition, to model clear routines in-person, a teacher can directly show what they look like through modeling physical actions. Yet, in a digital online setting, teachers must model routines through navigating digital interfaces within their EdTech tools. Furthermore, with every model of a digital routine, each one can be recorded and placed on the LMS for students to have the ability to view.

Third, when speaking about engaging students in routines centered around learning, teachers can create multiple exposures of knowledge for students like note-taking, summarizing, and non-linguistic representation (i.e., articulating their thoughts visually or using technology to create visual graphics and representations of learning) (Anthony, 2019; Marzano, 2003). This idea can also be connected with developing routines centered around technology utilized in the classroom. For example, each of these routines related to exposing students to content and engaging them in multiple facets of learning appears differently within in-person and digital classroom spaces. Note-taking may take place on an interactive slide, Microsoft OneNote, or on a Google Doc versus note-taking in person on a piece of paper. Also, when thinking about utilizing technology, routines need to be developed as to how students use the technology as an engagement tool for learning. Students need to have routines built around these multiple mechanisms of exposure to content and skills, which need to be crafted over time as new tools are introduced.

Fourth, routines must be intentionally designed within the online LMS as well as in the physical classroom. From accessing assignments and tasks to supports and resources, each of these spheres needs to be organized so students can navigate the various tools they must utilize to be successful in the classroom. Organizing in-person and digital classroom spaces relates to teacher clarity and designing coherent instructional plans (Anthony, 2019; Hattie, 2012). Within an LMS, content can be organized in a variety of ways ranging from the unit theme, week of school, and type of assignment/task. In contrast, within a physical classroom, different parts of the classroom may be organized based on the content, location of materials, technology, or by visuals and displays. Each must be taken into consideration in modern classroom settings. Therefore, using the LMS to create routines streamlines organization for students. Make it the one-stop-shop for accessing important tasks, assignments, materials, technology, and resources/supports that students may need.

Taken altogether, each of these facets of constructing routines in digital and in-person settings can help create classrooms that students can navigate within multiple spheres. Ultimately, when developing these routines, we must be intentional in what we are designing and modeling for our students while in-person and in digital spaces. If teachers are clear and direct with developing and modeling routines on a daily basis in both spaces, students can experience high levels of engagement and learning anywhere and at any time.

Instructional Strategy Integrations with EdTech for Setting Digital Classroom Routines & Norms

We will show you how to integrate various strategies to build routines into your LMS and the EdTech tools you utilize on a daily basis to amplify learning. Within this conversation, we will further outline step-by-step examples of how to marry both digital and in-person classroom routines and procedures. Each step is designed to engage your students while developing and implementing these routines over the course of the school day and year. Finally, to round out the chapter, there will be a conversation relating to citizenship within digital and in-person classroom spaces. This will focus on developing routines centered around cultivating a community of learners who are positive and safe in physical and digital classroom spaces. Overarching each of these three main topics discussed throughout the chapter are the ideas of efficiency, clarity, accessibility, organization, and personalization. All of these facets will be discussed within each topic on integrating routines with EdTech tools to nurture learning in all classroom environments.

LMS Integration

For any event to run smoothly, it is imperative that there are a few basic components met. For example, the event must be organized with clear insight as to how participants should interact. Those same participants should feel welcomed and comfortable to engage. It should meet the needs of all the individuals involved, and every single participant should be able to easily access the necessary materials or information to feel satisfied with the experience. The reality is that these principles aren't just applicable to events, but rather can be seamlessly applied to individual classrooms across the world. Just like any quality event includes essential elements of clarity, organization, personalization, efficiency, and accessibility for it to be considered exceptional, the same is true for our schools. Fortunately, an LMS acts as a hub in most classrooms and affords those same concepts for students and teachers.

Clarity

Educators everywhere understand the value of clarity and how it connects to student learning; if a teacher is clear in their directions, the student will be able to complete the assignment. If a student is clear in their articulation of frustration, the teacher can do everything in their power to support that student. When bridging the gap between synchronous and asynchronous time, the LMS becomes the most important tool to promote an environment grounded in clarity.

As a teacher begins their lesson for the day, the LMS is a great space to post their agenda. The agenda can act as a signpost that guides the rest of the class period. On this agenda, the students will understand the plan for the day, reflect on the objective they are trying to meet, and can revisit it after class to understand what asynchronous work they must complete before the next class period. Additionally, by posting a digital agenda on your LMS, an educator has the ability to hyperlink the assignments the students will be working on, thus making the search for materials easy; all students have to do is click on the hyperlink, and it can take them to their assignment for the day. Hyperlinks could be outside links, or even the custom assignment link from the LMS. For creative agenda templates, individuals can visit slidesmania.com, where Paula, the owner, has graciously provided customizable slides free to all educators.

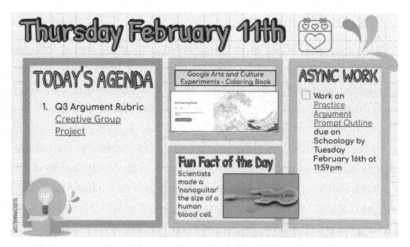

Figure 1.1 Digital Agenda - Template Adapted from Slidesmania.com

Additionally, most LMSs are equipped with a "task" or "to-do" area as well as a calendar. For every assignment that is posted in the LMS, these areas are also populated. Many educators are aware of these areas, but very few are deliberate about showing them to their students and really using them as a reinforcement for the outstanding assignments students must complete. To encourage student ownership over assignments, early in the semester, an educator can create a scavenger hunt that requires students to seek out all the different beneficial areas and beginning-of-the-year items in an LMS. For example, an educator could require the students to find: the course syllabus, how to contact their teacher, assignment due dates, procedures for turning in assignments, tasks/to-do lists, populated assignment calendar, message center, how to add an image, where to find notifications, the announcements vs. assignments areas, how to view your grades, et cetera The possibilities are endless; if a student learns how to navigate the LMS early on and the procedures are streamlined and remain the same throughout the year, there is no doubt that clarity will be the name of the game, thus promoting comfortability in approaching their own learning.

Organization/Efficiency

In order to promote efficiency throughout the year, there needs to be a clear structure of organization that permeates throughout your whole LMS; educators don't want to lose time while students aimlessly search for assignments. Students should be able to log in to the LMS and know exactly where to go to access the materials. There are a few organizational techniques an educator could use to support this endeavor.

First, depending on the LMS an individual is using, they should be mindful of organizing by folders or topics:

Figure 1.2 A QR Code to Examples of LMS Organization

https://bit.ly/12FigureIWO

If an educator is using an LMS with a folder-type organizational structure, they can create folders for each of their units, and when the unit is over, they can change the folder color to gray to denote that students should no longer reference the material in that folder. Color coding the folders gives a clear visual for students to follow when they are navigating the LMS and looking for current materials. If the LMS includes a topic-type organizational structure, the educator can clearly label the topic and add emojis to delineate which unit is current and those which no longer need to be interacted with; its as simple as adding an ✖ to the beginning of the topic for past units, and a ✅ for current ones. The topic titles are editable and can be changed as the educator sees fit.

Personalization

Just like a traditional classroom needs to be inviting, the same is true for the digital space. Educators can add a few different touches to their LMS to create a positive class culture for their students. This last year, the concept of a Bitmoji classroom exploded, and educators everywhere took advantage of all the wonderful materials that were openly shared. Creating a Bitmoji classroom not only adds a touch of personalization to the classroom, but also allows the educator to share a little bit about themselves in the process. If you are interested in creating your own Bitmoji classroom that you can add to your LMS, you can navigate to Facebook and search for the group "Bitmoji Craze for Educators." Individuals on that FB group have created templates that they are eager to share. If you are using Google Classroom, you can also create a Bitmoji banner that welcomes your students into the space; the ideal dimensions for a Bitmoji banner in Google Classroom is 1600 x 400 pixels. If you are using a platform like Schoology or Canvas, you can easily create a Bitmoji classroom that is hyperlinked and clickable using Google Slides, which can then be embedded into the LMS.

Figure 1.3 Examples of Bitmoji Classrooms Headers (*Dimensions for Google Classroom Bitmoji Classroom Banner: 16.67 x 4.17 inches*)

Example created with Google Slides. Page Setup: Widescreen 16:9

Anytime you can add a Bitmoji, emoji, or meme to your material, you are telling students that you are interested in bridging the gap between impersonal and personal and that you are eager to create a classroom where openness and sharing are important. Aside from the Bitmoji classroom being fun and inviting, it can also be practical and promote efficiency; if you link the course syllabus, orientation-type materials, or even zoom/meet links in your Bitmoji classrooms, students will be able to quickly access the materials thus maximizing the time in class that can be devoted to learning the material. If an educator does not want to go through the process of creating a full Bitmoji classroom, they can create hyperlinked buttons that act in a similar manner to the Bitmoji classroom.

Figure 1.4 Hyperlinked Buttons for Class Information

1.	Open a new Google Slides presentation
2.	Click file>page setup>click the dropdown box>custom
3.	Change the dimensions to 125 x 125 inches, press apply
4.	Click background > choose a background color or image, press done
5.	Click on the shape tool, and choose a curved corner box
6.	Add the shape to the slide, change the color using the fill tool
7.	Insert > word art > label the button however you would like > change the color using the fill and outline tools
8.	Duplicate the slide as many times as you want and change the button colors and font colors as you see fit
9.	Open a Google Doc and create a table that accounts for however many buttons you would like to use
10.	Navigate back to the Google Slide button presentation, right click on the slide (on the left panel, not the main panel) you want to copy > press copy or ctrl/cmd + C
11.	Navigate back to the Google doc, click in the first row of the created table, right click and press paste or ctrl/cmd + V - make sure you click paste unlinked
12.	Continue steps 10 & 11 until every button is added to the table on the google doc
13.	When table is populated, click on each individual button, find the link icon or push ctrl/cmd + K and add the hyperlink you want the button to forward to
14.	Once all buttons are hyperlinked, highlight the whole table, right click copy or press ctrl/cmd + C, navigate to your LMS, to post an update or announcement, and paste the buttons or press ctrl/cmd + V, then save

Table 1.1 How to Make Hyperlinked Buttons to Add to your LMS

Accessibility

The most important benefit of an LMS is that it provides ALL students the opportunity to access the class materials. When you integrate an LMS as part of the digital classroom routine, you are essentially giving students a landmark as they navigate and take ownership of their own learning. Every educator should err on the side of overcommunication in their classroom to ensure that each learner has the opportunity to be successful; an organized LMS allows for that overcommunication. Imagine if a student who struggles with an auditory processing disorder is left to fend for themselves as they approach a daily lesson. Yes, the teacher may have reviewed an agenda at the beginning of the class, pointed to the daily objective, and laid out the expectations for meeting that learning target, but if it is just audibly shared without being written or referenced anywhere, the student with the auditory processing disorder maybe picked up a quarter of the material that was referenced. Had the educator clearly voiced all the aforementioned, but the student knew they could also access it by looking at the LMS, they would be set up for much more success in the class. The same is true for the expression of asynchronous work at the end of the class period; many students fail to use a planner or calendar to map out their assignments upon leaving class. Educators often share the expectation for completing the homework at the end of the class period, but many students forget. If they can access the to-do list or the populated calendar on their LMS, they are more likely to complete the assignment and come prepared for the next class period.

In an effort to cater to the visual learner, screenshots and QR codes are great tools to keep all students on track. The beauty of the digital age is that technology continues to evolve and whereas a picture used to take days to develop, a simple screenshot photo can act as a clear indication of the expectations for the class. Imagine if a teacher wanted to ensure the visual learner had step-by-step instructions as to where to click to access material; the teacher could take a screenshot for every step, or even use an amazing tool called Iorad (https://www.iorad.com/) to guide every learner through the process. By laying out every step, there would be less confusion, and all learners would have an equal opportunity to manage their own learning processes. Additionally, the updated version of Google Chrome has integrated a built-in QR code generator that, with the click of a button in the URL bar, a teacher can access a QR code that can be added to an LMS and effectively guide the students to the expected website or page to access and complete their work; many students don't have Wi-Fi, and so, the QR code allows them to use cell phone data to access the material with a simple snap of the code.

Individuals often think of an LMS as a space that simply houses materials, assignments, and announcements, but it is, in fact, so much more. The LMS, if clearly organized, gives each and every student the scaffolded support they might need to approach the class with confidence, thus amplifying their learning and understanding of the material and propelling them toward success.

Marrying Digital and In-Person Classroom Routines that Blend Together

Classrooms are built on relationships and run on routines. Routines and procedures, like everything else in education, have adapted and evolved as classrooms have moved away from the traditional setting and now incorporate digital and blended aspects into everyday instruction. Most, if not all, classroom routines can be adapted and applied regardless of the learning environment. For example, today's students still need to turn in assignments. Routines are established at the beginning of the year that show them where and how to do so. Teachers have been distributing information and resources since the advent of the classroom. The methods for distribution have changed, but routines are still established. Today's teachers *and* students have had the experience of working in both in-person and digital learning environments. They, most likely, are comfortable moving between the two, and many routines have become blended through that process.

Classroom Norms

Every classroom, digital or in-person, runs best when classroom norms are clear and consistent. At the beginning of the year, establish these expectations together as a class. When the students take part in creating the class norms, they are more personalized, and the students take more ownership over their behaviors and the overall running of the classroom. To ensure these norms provide the clarity the students need, create them on a shared PowerPoint or Google Slide deck. The teacher can be the scribe as the community of learners offers suggestions. This initial discussion connects the learners more quickly to the new classroom. Once the final slide deck is created, it gets posted on the LMS and/or class website for easy access throughout the school year.

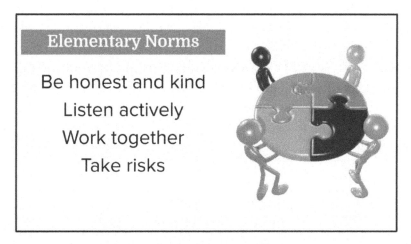

Figure 1.5 Example of Elementary Class Norms

Secondary Norms

Be present
Listen actively
Collaborate with ideas
Take risks
Be honest & kind
Be critical, don't criticize
Be vulnerable

Figure 1.6 Example of Secondary Class Norms

Once the norms are established for whole class work time, norms for small group work also need to be created. Again, this is a whole class discussion for students to give input on what makes teams operate successfully. As part of the small group expectations, teachers need to designate specific roles for each student while working in these groups. The individual responsibilities of each role need to also be clearly defined and posted in the room and/or on the small group norm slide deck. When students get to work in collaborative groups, it's helpful for the teacher to link the slide deck with small group norms and student roles in the lesson assignment. One of the first parts to beginning a new collaborative project, students should be required to review the norms and choose roles in order to be set up for success as a team.

Collaborative Norms

Choose your jobs
Take turns
Do your part
Be honest and kind
Listen actively
Work as a team

Figure 1.7 Example of Collaborative Norms

In some classrooms, it may be beneficial for the teacher and some students to role-play what those norms look like in small groups and create a screencast of the actions. The slide deck, along with the screencast, can provide quick reminders to students who might forget those norms in the moment. When teachers spend time modeling, it accesses a variety of learning modes to better reach all learners. Modeling has also been shown to promote more seamless transitions, requiring less time away from instruction. Clear and consistent norms also provide students with more time engaged in collaborative learning than those in classes without established routines (Cameron et al., 2008; Fisher et al., 2020).

Student Roles

Student roles can be job-based or content-based, where each student researches a different aspect of the assignment. In classrooms where learners aren't used to choosing their own roles, it helps for the teacher to assign them for the first few projects until they've had a chance to try out different jobs. When students are empowered to choose a role that falls within their skill sets, they are more likely to engage at a higher level as team members.

Figure 1.8 Examples of Job-based Student Roles

Getting students involved in as many areas of the classroom routines is the best way to personalize their instruction. In classes that blend in-person students and virtual students, teachers may want to consider integrating the two environments when providing collaborative work time. Students can collaborate through video conferencing apps and collaborative EdTech tools like Google, Office Online, and Adobe Express.

Home/School Connection

One of the positives that emerged from teaching through a pandemic was the increase in connection and communication between school and home. Teachers have reported higher percentages of parents checking the LMS and having a higher awareness of the curriculum and instruction in the classroom than in prior years. They feel more comfortable emailing the teacher to ask questions so that they can better support their children's learning at home. Similarly, many building leaders have touted the benefits of video conferencing for parent meetings, particularly those for IEPs. More parents are able to attend school meetings via video chat since the commute time is eliminated. Many of these practices will be continued post-pandemic after the clear benefits have been experienced. Platforms like Zoom, Microsoft Teams, and Google Meet provide easy access to meetings to promote the home/school connection.

Citizenship in a Digital and In-Person Classroom

Citizenship is not a new concept in classrooms. How to be a good citizen has been taught for centuries in school buildings. Digital citizenship, however, has only become mainstream in the last decade. There are actually many schools that still haven't adopted a digital citizenship curriculum. If students have digital devices, however, they need to be provided with the instruction and resources to know how to use them accurately, efficiently, and safely. The components of being a good citizen -- contributing to the community, accountability, honesty and integrity, courtesy, and respect for others -- are the same characteristics in the digital realm as they are in the physical classroom. Many of the aforementioned norms should direct students toward good citizenship behavior. Most students, however, need more intentional guides on being upstanding digital citizens.

The modern student doesn't know a life where digital devices and easy online access don't exist. While they have been raised in the digital era, they don't naturally know how to use technology for learning. They are pros at accessing various resources for entertainment and socialization, but teachers need to teach them how to use them safely and to further their own learning. Common Sense Media (https://www.commonsensemedia.org/) provides free teacher-created lesson plans for every grade band, covering every aspect of digital citizenship. The resources (e.g., slide decks, videos, formative assessments) are already created and part of the lesson plan. It's the easiest way to integrate high-quality digital citizen instruction into regular classroom learning. Everything from copyright use and password protection to staying safe on social media is covered. In addition to the resources provided for teachers, there is a parent component to the website where caregivers can access video game and movie reviews, along with other valuable materials to help teach good digital citizenship at home.

Figure 1.9 9 Digital Citizenship Themes

The importance of consistency in classroom routines was already mentioned. While Common Sense Media is fantastic for structure and delivery, teaching good citizenship qualities can't stop at the end of each lesson. There are easy ways to carry those practices into every lesson through the vocabulary the teacher models and quick teachable moments as they occur. Platforms such as Google Slides, PowerPoint, Sway, and Adobe Express provide image searches directly inside the app. These platforms only provide images that are copyright free to use. Teaching students to search for images inside these apps instead of doing a basic Google image search ensures that they are practicing good digital citizenship skills according to fair use policies. The teacher should remind students of this each time they create a multimedia presentation.

Collaborative documents and slide decks are great spaces in which entire classes or small groups can work or create. Invariably, however, someone will type something inappropriate, or edit or delete someone else's work. This provides a great teachable moment about accountability and respecting others' work. Both Microsoft and Google contain "version history" that allows any user to see who made changes and when. This also helps when these changes are accidental, as the teacher can revert to an earlier version and recoup the lost material.

Today's students spend a high amount of time on digital devices, both at school and at home. Because of that, teaching students to be good citizens in the classroom and in the larger community is something that should be intentionally taught, as well as integrated into daily discussions and lessons.

CONCLUSION—CLASSROOM ROUTINES WITHOUT BOUNDARIES

Throughout this chapter, we have seen that routines now span both in-person and digital realms. This means we must be intentional in designing our classroom routines to meet the needs of our students in both of these spaces. Some routines may encompass both in-person and digital spheres, while some will remain specifically geared toward in-person physical spaces or digital online spaces. Ultimately, digital and in-person routines are here to stay. Thus, as we navigate the future, the blending between each of these spaces with a classroom will only become more pronounced.

Routines hold together the fabric of our instruction and classroom culture. Underlining each is the notion of individual citizenship and what it means to not only be a student in a physical classroom environment but also in digital realms where instruction and learning take place. Teaching our students routines and how to navigate our classroom spaces as a citizen in a community of learners help optimize your instruction and magnify learning.

We must be judicious with teaching our students routines in both in-person and digital classroom spaces. Like various parts of the physical classroom, such as the front board, teacher's desk, the doorway, the side bookshelves, and physical paper assignment bins, the LMS holds many of the same functions. Our routines should center around delivering instruction, communicating with students, developing personal connections, and navigating how the class is organized. Additionally, our routines should be gradually built over time and consistently modeled. Whether it's using an EdTech tool, navigating the LMS, entering and exiting the classroom, an edu-protocol, or acting appropriately as a classroom citizen in-person during a class discussion, they must be reinforced and structured within the course of our lessons.

Altogether, classroom routines help establish positive learning environments that create the foundation for instruction to be delivered to students. With this said, routines will evolve over time. Routines will be added and subtracted from in-person and digital spaces. But, our ability to craft, model, and reinforce routines will be the catalyst to increasing student learning. Every instructional strategy integrated with EdTech is held together by the routines we establish. Therefore, as we progress throughout this book, always think back to our routines as the foundation of everything we do in classrooms.

CONTINUING THE CONVERSATION—I USED TO THINK VS. NOW I THINK

Directions: After completing Chapter One, reflect on digital classroom routines. What did you "used to think" and outline what you "now think" after reading the chapter and reflecting on your practice? Share your thoughts with your PLN with the hashtag #InstructWithoutBoundaries.

I Used to Think	Now I Think

CHAPTER 2
STUDENT ENGAGEMENT IN CLASSROOMS WITHOUT DEFINED BORDERS

Within any classroom setting, engagement is one of the most difficult enigmas for teachers and students to navigate. No student likes being in a quote, unquote "boring class." Teachers also want their students to be active learners in their classrooms. We want our lessons to be exciting yet full of breadth when it comes to the skills and content students are learning. What does this look like in the classroom? Engagement is complex within a classroom setting, but ultimately does not need to be.

There are many challenges when it comes to engaging students in modern classroom settings. For example, space and environment have become a reality that educators have to navigate as they plan for and deliver lessons. These days, many students and teachers find themselves teaching and learning both in traditional face-to-face as well as virtual classroom settings. Recently, classroom spaces have shifted to include online, blended, concurrent, and traditional in-person classroom experiences; while most individuals have to deal with one environment during a school year, so many individuals have experienced a combination of the aforementioned throughout the course of a single year. Each of those spaces and environments comes with its own difficulties and distractions. For instance, traditionally, a lesson might be interrupted by your occasional fire alarm, office aide, or phone call from the office; in modern classrooms, especially those that include virtual learning, a lesson could be interrupted for both the teacher and student by a disconnection due to a spotty WiFi signal, the whining of a child or sibling, or even the reality of an unwanted phrase, word, or sound due to the "almost quick enough" hit of that mute-all button. In addition to a shift in space/environment, relational and behavioral challenges arise, especially when classrooms are entirely online.

Unfortunately, teaching through a computer screen has resulted in less personal connections between teachers and students, and for many learners, personal and collective accountability is difficult to muster. Many books written about education will devote space to the power of building relationships; it is an integral aspect of any classroom. However, due to frequent space changes and the dreaded black screen, relationships and connections have been harder to cultivate. When learners are asked to toggle between virtual and in-person learning, motivation is disrupted, and that often leads to students checking out much quicker than they have traditionally; when students are checked out, their investment wavers, thus leading them to refrain from sharing the truest parts of themselves in the class setting. They attend class to check a box, and that is the extent of it. For virtual learners, many students have voiced the uneasiness that comes with the fact that all of their peers can just "stare at them," and so they choose to turn their cameras off due to insecurity; additionally, many black screens are the result of minimal bandwidth to support the strain of video conferencing. When a student can hide behind a black screen, it is challenging to hold them accountable, check for understanding, or build those sincere relationships that every educational scholar dictates are essential to each classroom. If relationships cannot be sufficiently built and motivation continually wanes, students are less likely to engage with the content. For example, if teachers cannot get to know their students and checks for understanding aren't sufficient, it is not likely that they are providing enough differentiation or personalized learning experiences, thus minimizing ownership of learning and leading to boredom.

Passive learning experiences without differentiation or personalization cause students to check out. Modern educational challenges present difficulties, but they have also made it clear that modern education solutions are more necessary than ever if we want to ensure we are providing limitless opportunities for all learners. Therefore, in an effort to address the issues, it is imperative that educators figure out ways to increase student engagement. Although there is no perfect answer, with the right combination of deliberately integrated instructional strategies and well-chosen EdTech tools, the level of engagement students may experience in a classroom setting can be taken to new levels; these ingredients will push beyond contemporary challenges that educators face and afford students the opportunity to create, collaborate, and problem solve in novel and engaging ways.

Our goal in this chapter is to demonstrate multiple research-based strategies to engage students in any class setting. We will unpack the research followed by illustrating the strategies. Then, we will integrate these strategies with readily available mainstream EdTech tools to illustrate the strategy, which then will boost student learning. By the end of this chapter, you will be able to take one or more of these strategies and incorporate them into your instructional design to engage students by building relationships, being intentional in your lessons, providing opportunities for students to be co-creators in their learning, and gamifying their experiences.

THE RESEARCH AND STRATEGIES—STUDENT ENGAGEMENT AND LEARNING

As we begin discussing engagement more in-depth, the research relating to what student engagement looks like within a classroom setting can be complicated, but very insightful as we unpack it and plan to integrate instructional strategies along with EdTech tools to expand student learning. The goal will be to focus on defining engagement as well as its elements and components. After reading the research on engagement, you will see how its components relate to active learning, which is key to think about as you begin evaluating and selecting the instructional strategies to implement within your classroom. To finalize our discussion on engagement research, a conversation will be provided regarding external factors within a classroom setting and beyond that may affect student engagement.

Ultimately, you will have the framework to begin evaluating the strategies and EdTech integrations we illustrate throughout this chapter for your classroom and students. This will go a long way as there will be many strategies and EdTech integrations for you to review and think about what will work best for your students and classroom after you are done reading this chapter.

Defining Engagement

Student engagement can be broken down into several elements within a continuum. Lim (2004) defined engagement as a number of behavioral, cognitive, or affective indicators across a continuum that can be observed by teachers when they see the effort and energy of students within a learning environment. These engagement indicators are widely accepted dimensions that promote student learning. First, we have cognitive engagement, which relates to the facets of self-regulation, deep learning, and understanding (Fredericks, Blumenfeld, & Paris, 2004; Fredricks, Filsecker, & Lawson, 2016). What this looks like in a classroom is a student's executive functioning, critical thinking, and understanding of classroom routines and norms. Second, we have affective engagement, which is interconnected with positive reactions to the learning environment by students to teachers and students to students (Fredericks et al., 2004; Fredericks et al., 2016). Ultimately, this is associated with having a positive social climate and community within a classroom setting. Students and teachers can create positive connections and relationships, which establish a safe and positive learning environment for students. In this instance, this indicator focuses on the collective atmosphere of a classroom, which affects the level of engagement of students. Last, we have behavioral engagement, which is related to positive conduct, participation, and persistence (Fredericks et al., 2004; Fredericks et al., 2016). This is centered at the individual level of the student because it relates to their individual actions.

When diving deeper into the indicators of cognitive, affective, and behavioral engagement, there are a number of examples of what they look like in practice. Bond and Bedenliner (2019) created a framework where each indicator of the concept of student engagement is separated into categories of engagement that make up actions, perceptions, and thought processes that occur in a classroom environment by students. Cognitive engagement relates to a student's ability to focus, self-regulate, follow through, have positive perceptions of self and self-efficacy, deep learning, and critical thinking (Bond & Bedenliner, 2019). For effective engagement, the sense of belonging, interest, excitement, sense of connectedness to school, positive attitude, relevance, and feeling appreciative all relate to this indicator (Bond & Bedenliner, 2019). Behavioral engagement can be broken down into effort, attendance, task completion, confidence, interaction, identifying opportunities, time on task, support and encouraging peers, and participation within a classroom setting (Bond & Bedenliner, 2019). Having each indicator further defined helps us determine how to align instructional strategies with them. There are many different actions and variables across a classroom setting we must consider. Thus, when thinking of student engagement as we progress through this chapter, keep these three indicators of engagement in mind and their characteristics as we discuss instructional strategies that focus on each. Overall, the goal is to ensure the instructional strategies that we outline and integrate with EdTech cover cognitive, affective, and behavioral student engagement.

Active Learning

As we think about the three main types of engagement and their characteristics, there is a concurrent term we often see, which is called active learning. Active learning essentially relates to a student's ability to develop a social construction of knowledge (Dewey, 1938). The concept of active learning is intertwined with the constructivism theory of knowledge that outlines how knowledge can be constructed and created within the mind of the learner versus being transferred directly from a teacher to a student (Bodner, 1986). Therefore, within classroom settings, the instructional design provides opportunities for students to have learning experiences that are based on overt and covert acts of communication. Communication in this sense can be verbal and written, which can take place on many different types of digital EdTech interfaces. Ultimately, the goal of active learning is to create a student-centered learning environment within our classroom and lesson design where students take the lead in their learning versus a teacher-centered approach. Avoiding instruction like teacher-led direct instruction is key to this thought process. Teachers are facilitators, and chunking their direct instruction into small segments helps create classrooms where students are co-pilots and pilots that drive their learning.

As we design opportunities for active learning within our classrooms, we need to focus on being facilitators of the instructional strategies. This means that teachers cannot engage in any prolonged direct instruction. Any form of teacher-facilitated instruction must be short and built into a strategy. It can be scaffolded and chunked, but not the main component of the strategy. Therefore, our primary focus when thinking about active learning and engagement should be focused on delivering strategies that are collaborative, cooperative, communication-based, inquiry-based, and problem-based. Additionally, forms of technology-enhanced learning further create opportunities for active student engagement and learning (Michael, 2006). In summary, these types of learning tasks put an onus on the learner and give them responsibility for what is learned (Alioon & Delialioğlu, 2019; McCabe & Conner, 2014).

Moving forward, think about the cognitive, affective, and behavioral aspects of student engagement and the characteristics of each that were discussed earlier. We can now take those characteristics of student engagement and think about strategies, activities, and tasks in our lessons that are centered around active learning. For example, affective and cognitive engagement can occur in tandem when synthesized with forms of active learning. As teachers, we can put our students in situations where they collaborate on a task within a structured group setting. Within this collaborative group setting and task, students can build a sense of belonging, community, and relevance. The task is concept mapping as they brainstorm about several predictions being made over a text they are reading. By completing this task, students are engaged in deep learning and critical thinking. Altogether, many forms of engagement are taking place. If we think about this as we select and integrate various strategies into our lesson, our students have a high chance of being engaged in active learning regardless of the classroom setting.

Other Factors to Consider: The Bioecological Student Engagement Framework

Beyond defining student engagement, we must see how many interconnected factors within a student's classroom environment affect their level of engagement. As teachers, we need to be aware of what can be affecting a student's level of engagement because the strategies we incorporate within our classroom may have to be tinkered with and adjusted based on the factors that influence your classroom and students. To explain this in detail, the bioecological student engagement framework by Bond and Bedenliner (2019) reveals what factors may influence student engagement. This framework is built upon Schwab's (1973) curriculum redevelopment framework by Bond and Bedenliner (2019) to demonstrate the interconnected dimensions of curriculum, students, teachers, family, technology, and other external factors affecting student engagement. Teachers must be aware of each of these external factors within their classroom as they think about the engagement strategies they plan to implement within their classroom. Being aware of what's going on in our classrooms and students' lives helps inform our practice as we will then be able to weigh strategies and EdTech tools that work best for our students and setting.

Specifically, for this book, an emphasis must be on the learning environment and technology affecting student engagement as our goal is to amplify learning with instructional strategies to increase engagement and learning but also to extend it further with an EdTech tool integration. When thinking of how technology affects a learning environment, Bond and Bedenliner (2019) describe how the incorporation of EdTech affects teachers, students, the classroom environment, the technology itself, and the activities and tasks we ask our students to complete. Based on how the technology affects each of these factors, it then impacts the affective, cognitive, and behavioral indicators of student engagement. Therefore, each factor must be considered as it can influence how our students engage in their learning environment. For example, if the class is online for a synchronous online class session, how does the instruction being conducted via a virtual meeting tool like Zoom, Google Meet, or Microsoft Teams alter the student learning environment? Our students' learning environment is shaped by the virtual meeting platform itself by chat feature, screen sharing, polling, and more. Furthermore, this all determines how teachers and students interact with the activities integrated with the technology.

Instructional Strategy Integration with EdTech Tools to Amplify Learning: Engagement

Since we now have a background in conceptualizing what student engagement looks like within a classroom setting as well as the external factors affecting it, let's focus on the strategies we are going to discuss that foster student engagement. With this in mind, as each strategy is discussed throughout the rest of the chapter, we also focus on how that strategy can be integrated with various EdTech tools to foster student learning. Our strategies for this chapter will relate to four themes of instructional strategies that interrelate with cognitive, affective, and behavioral indicators of engagement:

1. Building Connections with Students
2. Intentional Design
3. Students are Co-Creators of Knowledge - Conceptual Mapping and Prediction
4. Gamified Learning

Each of these themes of interwoven instructional strategies and EdTech integrations creates opportunities for our students to be engaged in learning within any classroom setting. We ultimately want to provide our students with many opportunities to be engaged. From building a classroom community, providing active learning scenarios, developing student agency and ownership in their learning, to gamifying learning, the opportunities are limitless as we now have the strategies and technology to transform student engagement and learning.

As you progress through the remainder of the chapter, there will be a number of examples outlining several strategies found within each theme of interwoven strategies and EdTech integrations. Examples will involve a step-by-step outline of each strategy along with how it can be integrated with EdTech tools. Various areas of content will be used as examples of how the strategies discussed can be employed across a variety of different disciplines and grade levels. The goal of each strategy and EdTech integration is to demonstrate they can be used in any classroom setting, for any grade level, and in any area of content. We want teachers to know each strategy and integration is flexible and can be adjusted to any setting. Now, let's dive further into learning more about each strategy and EdTech integration. Each is designed to create multiple modalities of engagement for your students. Taken altogether, you will have a toolkit of engagement strategies integrated with EdTech after you have completed reading about each theme of interwoven engagement strategies.

Engaging Students by Building Connections

Deep learning rarely occurs until foundational relationships have been formed. The teacher can implement strategies beginning on the first day of the school year to get to know each student and build trust. A fun idea to begin with on that first day is 2 Truths and a Lie. Using Google Slides or PowerPoint Online, the teacher creates a slidedeck with enough slides for each student in the class. The teacher shares the collaborative slide deck with the directions for students to type their names on their assigned slide (elementary teachers may want to already have names listed on the top of individual slides to reduce confusion) and then choose three images that represent them. Two of the images are true, and one is false. Taking turns, each student introduces themselves verbally and tells their three things, pretending that each is true. The rest of the class tries to decide which is the lie. This is a fun, low-pressure way of working in a collaborative slide deck and an easy way for teachers to start gathering information about their new students.

1. In Google Drive, go to +New and select Google Slides
2. Choose the default "Simple Light" or Simple Dark" Theme
3. Title it "2 Truths and a Lie"
4. Make Slide 1 your title slide
5. Make Slide 2 your directions slide. Include these simple directions:
   a. Add your first and last name to your assigned slide
   b. Click on "Insert" in the menu bar and select "Image"
   c. Click on "Search the web"
   d. Search for images that tell us about you and one that could be about you
   e. Choose three to insert onto your slide
   f. Resize them by clicking on one corner and zooming in or out
   g. Do not edit the Theme of the slide deck or anyone else's slide
6. Create enough "Title Only" slides for each student in your classroom.
7. Decide if you are going to go ahead and type each person's name at the top of a slide (if so, change the first step in your directions to "Find the slide with your name on it"), or if you will just assign them a slide number.
8. Share the Google Slide presentation with your students via the link in your learning management system, or via email.
9. When everyone is finished, project the finished presentation and have each student share their information while asking their peers to discover the lie.

*Note: you will likely have students type on someone else's slide during this activity. Assume positive intent and use it as a teachable moment. You can even demonstrate going to "File" and "Version History" to show students how you revert to a previous version. Often, students change the theme, thinking they are changing the background of just their slide. You can use this as a teachable moment, as well, showing how to change the background of just one slide.

Table 2.1 Step-by-Step Directions in Setting up 2 Truths and a Lie Using Google Slides. (**Note:** *This strategy can easily be converted into PowerPoint Online if you are in a Microsoft District.*)

A more formal method of gathering information is the use of personal interest surveys. These can be quickly created in Google or Microsoft Forms and shared with students to complete. Since both of these tools populate spreadsheets, teachers can sort for commonalities among their students. Using the information from the surveys allows teachers to personally connect with students and incorporate student interests into teaching and learning. As relationships are formed, and interests are acknowledged, student engagement naturally increases.

1. In Google Drive, go to +New and select Google Forms
2. Give it a catchy title about getting to know them
3. Write your first question (i.e. What do you prefer to be called?) and then click the + sign in the sidebar menu.
4. Continue with age-appropriate questions that will give you a glimpse into their likes, passions, interests, and dislikes.
5. Make the questions as fun as possible
6. You can change the look of the form by clicking the paint palette icon in the top right-hand corner of the form.
7. Click "Send" and share with the students via the learning management system or via email.
8. As they start submitting responses, click on "Responses" at the top of the form and click on the green square in the top corner to create a new spreadsheet.
9. After the spreadsheet is created, you can sort the information by clicking "Data" in the menu bar.

Table 2.2 Provides Step-by-Step Directions for Setting up a Personal Interest Survey in Google Forms.

Building relationships is an ongoing endeavor. Teachers need to continuously find ways to make personal connections with students. After the beginning of the school semester, regular check-ins are important. These check-ins can be created in Forms, again, or could be quick messages through your learning management system or email. These check-ins are usually more effective in relationship building when they aren't school/class-related. When students know that their teachers are invested in them, they are more likely to invest in the class. In person, these can even take on quick conversations as students are coming in and leaving your room. In a virtual world, you can use breakout rooms for quick check-ins, or a video-recording resource like Flipgrid.

Engaging Students with Intentional Design

Teachers are similar to singers and songwriters. They design the lesson *and* they teach it. This puts teachers in a unique position of knowing their content, knowing their students, and being able to create lessons in a way to engage all learners through intentional design. It's been said that the "sage on the stage" (i.e., someone who spends the period lecturing) should have transitioned to the "guide on the side" at this point. And yet, far too many educators are still doing the majority of the talking during class. The modern educator has the responsibility to prepare their students for every opportunity after leaving that class. Through intentional design, teachers can empower students to not only be engaged in their learning, but to be self-motivated to pursue it.

Teachers should be planning for limited lecture time. Some call this process chunking, while others prefer to refer to it as mini-lessons. An easy guide is to go by the average age of the students in the class. If you teach second-graders, your mini-lessons shouldn't last longer than seven or eight minutes. If you teach seniors, you might be able to get away with lecturing for eighteen minutes. There are times when this method of direct teaching is necessary, but when it is, keep it as short in duration as possible, layering in multiple opportunities for active learning in the process. Writing lends itself to an easy illustration of chunking a lesson. The teacher can introduce or review a new writing concept during the mini-lesson, give students an opportunity to discuss it with a partner, and then spend a concentrated amount of time applying it in their personal writing projects. During that time, the teacher is free to have one-on-one or small group writing conferences, personalizing the instruction. Similarly, in a science lesson, the new content is taught (perhaps only one part of it), and then students apply it in a lab situation. The teacher may have three or four mini-lessons in one science period, but they are interrupted with periods of active learning to engage the students and allow for deeper learning to happen.

Active Engagement (concentrated time applying the new learning through discussion and practice): 20-40 minutes
This is the time for the teacher to meet one-on-one or with small groups to differentiate instruction.

Mid-lesson mini lesson (not every lesson needs an additional mini lesson) 5 minutes	Share/Assess (how will students demonstrate their learning?) 5-10 minutes

Figure 2.1 Template for a Lesson Plan Using the Chunking/Mini Lesson Framework

Lesson	Date
Resources:	Standards:
Teaching Point:	
Connection (connecting to prior knowledge): 1-2 minutes	
Teach/Model (direct teach one new concept/skill/strategy): 5-10 minutes	

Station-Rotation Model

The Station-Rotation Model is a framework that is utilized in classrooms and puts chunking into practice. This framework is a Blended Learning Model that integrates teacher-led stations (i.e., mini-lessons), collaborative activities and performance tasks, and an independent station (typically online) in one class period. The model allows for some differentiation and personalized learning opportunities, while chunking the entire lesson into the three stations keeping the learning active and engaging. This model can be used in face-to-face settings, as well as in virtual and blended learning environments. The independent station is done asynchronously by individual students. The collaboration station is done in small groups in person, in breakout rooms, or a combination of both. The teacher-led station is done in person at a small table off to the side of the room or in a virtual breakout room. Collaborative technologies like Office 365, Google Workspaces, Padlet, and Adobe Express make it easy to work together in the collaborative station. For the independent station, using adaptive software (if the school has purchased it) is a simple integration. If not, Hyperdocs are the perfect EdTech tool to utilize. The creators of Hyperdocs define them as "digital lesson plans that are designed by teachers and given to students. They provide access for students to all the content and learning in one organized digital space" (Hyperdocs.co, 2021). There is no reason to reinvent the wheel. The website, Hyperdocs.co, provides ready-made templates and samples that are easy to save to your Google Drive or download as a Microsoft document, saving educators so much time in the formatting of the lesson. The beauty in using a Hyperdoc is that it can be as individualized as needed for each student. The teacher provides the learning prompts, the resources, and the assignments for students to work through independently. There are many ways to offer multiple choices for knowledge construction and demonstrating learning on a Hyperdoc, also leading to more engaging opportunities for the students.

Engaging Students by Making Them Co-Creators of Knowledge—Conceptual Mapping

Most educators who have been in the classroom even just a few years can attest to the fact that encouraging students to meet teachers in the middle and assume the role of co-creator of knowledge is an effective strategy to enhance student learning. Educators everywhere celebrate when a student latches on to a concept, gets excited about the investigation, and exemplifies their learning in a new and creative way. Student engagement is vital for any classroom, and encouraging students to become co-creators of knowledge through the use of critical thinking activities and tools is a beneficial strategy for any classroom.

A concept is defined as "something conceived in the mind," a general or abstract thought or notion (Merriam-Webster, 2021). Traditionally, many educators rely on rote memorization when it comes to important concepts in their classrooms; while memorization has its place in education, it cannot be the sole strategy teachers use to ensure students are grasping the concepts, especially since it promotes more passive than active learning. Memorization is directly linked to remembering, which is mostly a passive process; in an effort to grow as learners, critical thinking needs to be at the core of the curriculum in order for true learning to take place. If a student cannot internalize the concepts, then they won't be able to transfer that learning at a later date which is the cornerstone exemplification of effective learning. Consider this—a typical elementary student has seven subjects they need to learn throughout a given week, and most high school students attend 6-7 classes over the course of the day; if educators are asking students to memorize the concepts in each of those classes without giving them the tools to solidify that learning into true understanding, they are setting themselves and their students up for disappointment. Most likely, the students will memorize the concepts to meet the immediate need and then forget the content when it is no longer needed; this doesn't bode well for subjects that rely on the building of concepts over the course of the school year. It would be more effective to provide activities and strategies that encourage deep internalization of the concepts they are studying. The reality is this, students often struggle to wrap their minds around more complex concepts, and it is up to educators to help them create a link between old and new knowledge; in an effort to increase a student's ability to learn and retain the necessary knowledge, concept mapping is an effective tool that gives students the opportunity to visualize the concept, thus making the understanding more meaningful and by default, enhances the retrieval process due to the connections that take place within that process. Many educational technology companies understand the importance of this process and therefore have created a variety of tools that will support educators as they plan to support their students in moving from passive remembering to active learning.

Interactive Slide Decks

One way to solidify concepts is to offer opportunities for categorizing, naming, or sorting. A great resource for this could be an interactive slide deck. This tool could be used in any setting — virtually, blended, or face to face. The idea is to use an add-on with your Google slide deck or Microsoft PowerPoint, such as Peardeck or Nearpod, and then push it out to your students via your LMS. Using interactive slides, you can virtually enhance any process of conceptual thinking. The goal is to start with individual concepts, solidify understanding of the basics, then move students to start seeing patterns and making connections.

For example, in order to understand individual concepts, the first step might be to build student vocabulary; in an effort to support this process, you can encourage students to provide examples and non-examples of the concept using a Frayer model chart combined with an interactive slide deck. You can push this slide deck out to each student using your LMS and evaluate in real-time whether or not the students understand the concepts.

Figure 2.2 QR of an Illustration of What a Frayer Chart Would Look Like
Both Empty and Filled In

https://bit.ly/22FigureIWB

With a little app-smashing by using two EdTech tools in a sequence to implement a strategy, you can set this interactive slide up. Using Google Drawings, you can create a simple Frayer Chart template with the vocabulary word listed, save it, then add it as a background image to your slide deck. From there, you can open your Peardeck add-on and add a "text" addition to each chosen slide (*see* Figure 2.3 for step-by-step directions).

1. In Google Drive, go to +New and select Google Drawings
2. Using the shapes tool, add all the necessary shapes to create the Frayer Chart (area for vocabulary word in middle, segmented into 4 sections)
3. Save an image copy of Frayer Chart to your Drive or desktop by clicking File>Download >.jpg
4. Open a new Google Slide by typing the shortcut into your URL bar: slides.new
5. Click on Background > choose image > Browse to find Frayer Chart and upload
6. Add Pear Deck Add-on to Google Slides
   a. Click Add-ons > Get Add-ons > search Pear Deck for Google Slides Add On > install
7. Once added, Open Pear Deck Add-on to begin making slides interactive
   a. Click Add-ons > Pear Deck for Google Slides Add-on > Open Pear Deck Add-on
8. Once Pear Deck panel pops up on the right side of the screen, go to slide you want to make interactive and click the corresponding options under the heading "Ask Students a Question"

9. Slide will become interactive once you see the gray bar pop up on bottom of slide

Note: the gray bar might cover your chart, you can always click the gray bar and move it off the slide-- as long as it stays in the gray area near the slide, it will work

Figure 2.3 Step-by-Step Directions in Setting up a Frayer Model in Google Drawings, Adding it to a Slide Deck, and then Making it Interactive

You can also complete this same activity by creating an editable slide deck that students can collaboratively work on in real-time. For example, you can break students up into groups, assign one vocabulary word per group, provide edit access to the slide deck, and students can complete a vocabulary journal in the slide deck within small groups or breakout rooms, and then return and share their learning via presentation with the class. To extend the learning, you can encourage students to provide the rationale for examples and non-examples. This strategy can be modified for any classroom as well by changing the categories; for example, instead of "Definition, Characteristics, Examples, & Non-examples," you can change it to "Examples, Non-Examples, Essential Characteristics, and Non-Essential Characteristics," and it could be used for character development in the ELA classroom.

Additionally, as classrooms move from the study of individual concepts to more complex concepts, students can use Interactive Slides to make connections between those complex concepts. For example, if a class is studying plant and animal cells, they could use a Venn Diagram to make comparisons and identify contrasts between the concepts. Students can use a slide deck to add text, search images on the web and add them, or draw their own images to exemplify their understanding. You can take it a step further and provide a triple Venn Diagram if the concepts include the study of ancient civilizations such as the Mayans, Aztecs, or Incas (*see* Figure 2.4 below for examples).

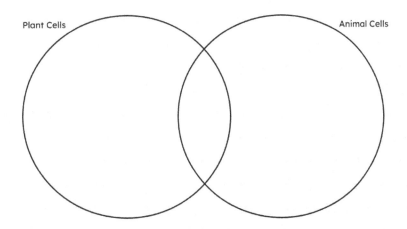

Figure 2.4 Visual Representation of How to Include Venn Diagrams to Make connections Between Concepts

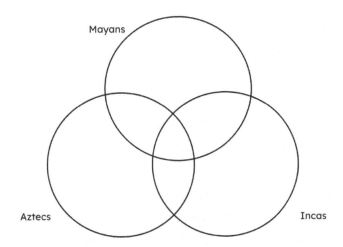

These images can be added as background to slide decks, and students can independently or collaboratively complete the diagrams. A teacher can watch this happen in real-time by toggling the view of the slide deck from the normal view to the grid view, which can be found at the bottom left of the side panel (it looks like a waffle). As students work, a teacher can monitor the work of each of their students in real-time.

Sketchnoting

Another effective method of concept mapping includes Sketchnoting. Sketchnoting is a visual note-taking strategy that allows students to make visual choices as they navigate through a concept. Sketchnoting essentially is characterized by Dual Coding Theory because it combines words and images to make meaning. In this theory, Paivio suggests that if an individual can store a concept in both the verbal and image memory, they are more likely to be able to retain the concept due to its storage in two memory areas over just one, as cited in Thomas (2014). The whole goal of Sketchnoting is for a student to follow along with what is being taught and solidify their understanding by honing in on key concepts and points, and visually exemplifying that understanding through a combination of images and words.

Sketchnoting can be done by hand or digitally, then uploaded to a slide deck for class sharing, or to an assignment on an educator's class LMS. This process does require some practice, but it allows students to create visual maps of learning that they can then look back on for reference. The structure is broken down into various containers, dividers, arrows, and lines. Sketchnoting can provide students an alternative method of note-taking while enhancing active participation more than a simple cloze-note process could.

The process of Sketchnoting asks students to slow down and consider the ways in which they can exemplify their learning in both image and word form. Google Drawings or Microsoft OneNote are great resources for this activity. Both platforms allow students to draw, sketch, or write notes with a digital pen or a mouse. There are also shape galleries on both platforms to support those students who are not interested in drawing freehand.

Consider the Water Cycle. If an educator wants their students to understand the different phases of the water cycle, they can give them an article to read, or provide them a page of notes, but with Sketchnoting, students can critically think about and make their own meaning of the process by completing a simple sketchnote. To extend this activity, a teacher could flip their class by assigning a video for students to watch on the Water Cycle, and students could come to class the next day with a sketchnote of their understanding that they can then explain to peers in a Pair-Share face-to-face or in a breakout room.

1. Open Microsoft OneNote and create New Section by clicking "add section" in bottom right of screen
2. Title New Section - Water Cycle Unit
3. Title Page - Steps of the Water Cycle
4. Begin Drawing by clicking Draw at the top of the screen. The following image represents the freehand options available:

Or... If students would rather use shapes, they can click Insert > Shape and choose from the variety of options that are listed:

Line	Elbow Double Arrow	Diamond
Arrow	Rectangle	2 dimensions, positive
Double Arrow	Oval	2 dimensions, full
Elbow	Triangle	3 dimensions
Elbow Arrow	Parallelogram	

5. Once they are finished with their sketchnote, they can click the share button in the right-hand corner and send the sketchnote to their teacher by adding their email, or copying a shareable link to upload to their LMS

Note: Additionally, students can collaborate in real-time with their peers by sharing their editable OneNote page. Also, students can add audio explanations to their page breaking down their sketchnote

Figure 2.5 Step-by-Step Directions for Students to Begin a Sketchnote for the Water Cycle in Microsoft OneNote

Some other available free Sketchnoting platforms include:

Web	Apple	Android
Google Jamboard Google Slides Google Keep AutoDraw Quick Draw Whiteboard.Chat	Affinity Designer Drawing with Carl Notability	Tayasui Sketches

Concept mapping includes many different components, and it can sometimes feel overwhelming, but building in opportunities for students to demonstrate their learning in a dynamic but structured manner will not only enhance the student learning, but it will also engage students as active participants. Educators every-where can attest to the power of creation and investigation. If a student has some independent or collaborative ownership over their own learning, they are more apt to remain engaged for the entirety of the lesson. Students can become co-creators of knowledge in the classroom, and there are various educational technology tools that can support educators and students alike in that process.

Engaging Students through Gamified Learning

In a world where external reinforcement is endless, educators have to adapt to ensure they are stimulating the very same pleasure centers that are continuously sparked by external stimuli. Fortunately, brilliant individuals tapped into the psychology of pleasure and motivation, and thus gamification became a trend in education. Gamification, grounded in game theory, is an effective strategy because research shows that if learners are having fun, they are more likely to be engaged with the content. There are a plethora of approaches to gamification being used across classrooms; however, some of the more popular ones include: Quiz-Style Games, Virtual Escape Rooms, and Digital Scavenger Hunts.

Quiz-Style Games

According to EdTechReview (2013), "Game-Based Learning is designed to balance subject matter with gameplay and the ability of the player to retain and apply said subject matter to the real world." When students log in to a Quizziz, Kahoot!, or Blooket, for example, their sole focus is to beat out the competition, and teachers are willingly endorsing this competitive nature because they have craftily created a platform for learning disguised in the form of a game. The beauty of a quiz-style game is it gives the students an opportunity to solve problems in context and provides immediate and actionable feedback that increases motivation and engagement while also optimizing learning.

For example, imagine that a Biology educator wants to start the class period with a review of the previous day's concepts surrounding atoms; they could give the students a pencil/paper recall quiz that encourages retrieval of concepts (and, in some instances, that could work), or they could take a page out of their students' favorite video games and navigate to Blooket.com, sign in with the SSO for Google, head to the "Discover" section, and search for "Atoms." Once they have completed that process, they would be provided various teacher-made examples that they could choose from, which could easily be shared with students by simply providing a link. This approach allows educators to reinforce the material from the previous day while also receiving clear data that maps the level of student understanding, thus allowing teachers to plan whether they can move forward, or need to stop and reteach. These quiz-style games can act as entrance/exit tickets and formative/summative assessments, in addition to encouraging the student to participate and remain engaged with the content in a way that builds intrinsic motivation (Song & Keller, 2001).

1. Navigate to Blooket.com
2. Click Sign Up in the right hand corner and sign up using your Google account or a different email
3. Once you are logged in, you will be brought to your teacher dashboard, navigate to the top of the screen and click the compass icon which will direct you to the Discover area (a library of all the Blookets available)
4. Search for a set using a keyword relevant to your lesson
5. Preview questions and if you are ready to use the Blooket, click the "Host" button in the right hand corner
6. Select a Game Mode (these game modes will structure exactly how competitors interact with their peers -- *Note: a favorite is "Gold Quest" where students can earn gold for right answers and then steal the earned gold from their peers; the student with the most gold at the end of a time frame, wins!)
7. Once you choose a game mode, it will give you details that will help you decide if that game mode is right for you. Once you are happy, click "Host Game"
8. Select the time limit and adjust any additional details for your purposes, then click "Host Now"
9. Students can then join the game in two ways:
   a. They can navigate to blooket.com/play and enter the Game ID, or
   b. Teacher can copy the "join link" by clicking "Copy Join Link" in the upper right corner of the screen and share that link with their students to log on

Figure 2.6 Step-by-Step Directions for Logging In, Searching for a Blooket, and Sharing It With the Class to Play

Virtual Escape Rooms

A virtual escape room is an effective engagement strategy because it is grounded in connection. These activities require the learners to make deep connections with the material in an effort to solve the puzzles; connections lead to ownership. If we add a puzzle to solve in the mix, then students will have the opportunity to explore and make their own meaning of the scenario, thus leading to ownership and engagement.

Creating a virtual escape room must happen in two phases: the brainstorming phase and the creation phase. Before an educator can unleash students to become digital sleuths, they need to set the purpose for the experience; this is best done by evaluating what measurable objective they would like their students to meet (Note: a good first step is backward mapping the skills you are interested in testing.) Once the objective is set, the educator can start to set the scene; this involves crafting an engaging and interesting story to captivate your audience. From there, it is time to brainstorm and write the puzzles, riddles, and clues that will guide the learners through the storyline and eventually lead them to break out and escape. When creating clues, teachers must ensure they are considering skill level, task, and time; students should be able to figure out the clue in a timely manner, or they will become frustrated and disengaged. After the brainstorming phase, it is time to move to the creation phase.

To begin the creation phase, it is important that educators pick a platform that they, and their students, are familiar with that will act as the virtual "room;" if a teacher attempts to use a new digital platform for the escape room and the students have not had a chance to engage with the platform previously, they are likely to lack the technical know-how to navigate the challenges an educator has established for them. Once a virtual "room" is chosen, the teacher can then create a series of digital locks; each puzzle will be solved to gain the numbers, letters, words, or phrases that will unlock each lock as they complete the challenges. Once all the "locks" are opened, the students will have effectively escaped the virtual escape room.

Digital Scavenger Hunts

Another effective method of investigation that encourages students to think quickly and offers an opportunity for choice and voice is a digital scavenger hunt. Digital scavenger hunts provide students the opportunity to seek out items and demonstrate their findings in the form of pictures or videos.

Digital Scavenger Hunts are largely used in classrooms to promote engagement, encourage fun, and as get-to-know-you activities, but they can also be content-based. The digital scavenger hunt is simple to put together and highly engaging; all an educator needs to do is consider which platform would work best to collect student evidence and what items they want the students to find or what tasks they want them to complete.

The following digital platforms act as appropriate platforms for students to display their findings:

- **A Slide Deck:** Each student could be assigned a blank slide deck that they add their picture/video evidence to and could even take it a step further and decorate their slide deck to share a little bit about their artifacts. Google Slides is a great resource if your students will be using a Chromebook to take their pictures; they can upload their pictures to their Google Drive and, from there, seamlessly add them to a Google slide deck. Teachers can individually assign this slide deck using their LMS of choice. If a woodshop teacher was planning to teach students how to measure and cut wood in the next class lesson, then the night before the lesson, they could ask students to find everyday items around their house that could act as measuring tools, and students can upload those pictures to a slide deck that could be used as a discussion starter the next day in class.
- **GooseChase** is an iOS and Android application that allows teachers to create custom scavenger hunt tasks, and students can upload videos/pictures directly using their phones. (In the cases where Wi-Fi is an issue, this is an alternative approach to keep individuals engaged because they can use their data plan instead.) When a student uploads an artifact to the challenge, the teacher can then approve the upload and award points to the students. Teachers can set a specific amount of time for gameplay, and the student that has the highest point value, in the end, is the winner.
- **Fliphunt:** Flipgrid is a platform that many educators use because it is simplistic, easy to navigate, and affords teachers easy organization by

allowing the teacher to enroll students into a group (which is the equivalent of a virtual classroom). Teachers can easily create a Fliphunt by generating a list of items they would like their students to find or tasks they need to accomplish. From there, students are given the link to the Fliphunt; they log in and record themselves carrying out the tasks assigned. Educators can add an extra layer of urgency by limiting the amount of time the students are given to record; for example, instead of having 5 minutes to take time to deliberate which item would best fit the requirement, they could be given a minute and a half and will need to pick up the pace in their processing. Flipgrid gives students the opportunity to add filters, text, stickers, borders, and more to decorate their pictures and videos. As an extension activity, the teacher could leave the Fliphunt unmoderated, and the students can navigate back into the topic after completing their own post and watch and comment on their peers' posts, thus making it a collaborative endeavor. This activity gives a tactical approach to an engaging experience and encourages students to think on their toes.

Gamification provides students with clear objectives that ultimately give the learning a purpose. Especially with the help of technology, gamification takes mundane tasks and encourages learning through play; it shifts the task from one of consumption to one of creation. As learners engage with various educational games, the process of the game structure and play will become more and more familiar; once they understand the ins-and-out of gameplay and in an effort to extend the depth of learning, the educator can ask the students to create their own quiz-style games, digital escape rooms, or digital scavenger hunts.

CONCLUSION—ENGAGEMENT IN CLASSROOMS WITHOUT DEFINED BORDERS

Throughout this chapter, a variety of different forms of student engagement strategies integrated with EdTech tools were discussed that are derived from research on student engagement. The research focused on engagement in the classroom and how active learning directly relates to engagement levels. Student engagement within any classroom setting can be achieved through several different avenues. For this chapter, the focus was on integrating engagement strategies related to building relationships, being intentional in your lessons, providing opportunities for students to be co-creators in their learning, and gamifying learning.

Strategies involving building relationships, creating student agency by being co-creators of their content, gamifying learning, and having the intentional design elements of student engagement create a plethora of opportunities for our students to participate in learning. When interwoven together throughout the course of the lesson, there is the opportunity to ensure many of the components and characteristics of active learning inside the cognition, affective, and behavior elements of student engagement come alive within the classroom.

All of these strategies are then integrated and extended by the use of EdTech. From interactive slides, forms, recording devices, Sketchnoting, and drawing tools, the opportunities for students to engage in the learning are offered in a multitude of ways. Ultimately, when coupled with the instructional strategies that are designed to heighten engagement, the integration of the strategy and EdTech tools heighten student engagement in any classroom setting. Regardless of whether the classroom setting is within an online, blended, concurrent, or traditionally in-person, these strategies and integrations can be utilized to enhance instruction and learning.

The implications of increasing student engagement are immense in today's world. The number of distractions increases in digital or blended learning settings. Those distractions are difficult to handle without pragmatic instructional integrations and set routines. Additionally, we have less student accountability and less personal connection with teachers and students within a class. However, with the instructional and EdTech integrations discussed in this chapter, the differentiation and personalization of student engagement as well as strategically planned active learning experiences create environments where students can thrive in modern classroom settings.

As we move forward, remember that each strategy and integration can be adjusted to your context and setting in education. Regardless of whether you teach elementary, secondary, or higher education, each strategy and integration outlined in this chapter can be adapted and adjusted to meet your needs as a teacher and your students. Going beyond this chapter, the strategies and EdTech integrations that were discussed can also be utilized in tandem with strategies you learn in other chapters throughout this book. Many of the best integrations can be sequenced together throughout the lesson you have designed. Therefore, synthesize the strategies and integrations as much as you can. The more that happens over the course of a lesson and unit, the more powerful learning will be for your students!

CONTINUING THE CONVERSATION— 3 - 2 - 1 FORMAT

Directions: After completing Chapter Two, what are three things you've learned, two questions you have, and one instructional strategy and EdTech integration you would like to implement in your classroom? Share your thoughts with your PLN with the hashtag #**InstructWithoutBoundaries.**

What are three things you have learned from this chapter?
What are two questions you may have after reading this chapter?
What is one instructional strategy and EdTech integration you would like to implement in your classroom after reading this chapter?

CHAPTER 3
STUDENT COLLABORATION WITHIN CLASSROOMS THAT TRANSCEND BOUNDARIES

A simple internet search will reinforce the idea that the most high-functioning and effective teams are made up of individuals that possess a certain set of skills or qualities that contribute to that team's success; those skills might include effective communicators, creative problem-solvers, and critical thinkers, but, without a doubt, every search will note the power of being an effective collaborator. If students can seamlessly and effectively engage with their peers, they will gain a greater chance of success as they enter college and/or the workforce. As we prepare students for jobs that do not yet exist, we have to remember that the development of leadership qualities is just as important as the content we teach. So, in an effort to meet the demands of future industries, we must prepare today's students to be lifelong learners that can communicate, cooperate, and collaborate with others. As education continues to shift, we have to keep in mind that we live in a world where students may not always see their classmates or colleagues in-person, so we must teach our students not only how to collaborate with others face-to-face, but digitally as well.

Within our instruction, we may find it difficult at times for students to speak and interact with others. Challenges arise when we begin an activity that is geared toward student interaction and collaboration, but ends with students communicating minimally and working independently on the task. As with digital classroom routines, when thinking about student collaboration, we should build in routines and strategies that, over time, will develop into engaging, collaborative opportunities for students to learn. With any form of instructional shift, we are developing a culture where these shifts become normal for students as well as teachers. Collaboration can be one of the more difficult shifts because it takes time, and it is a cultural shift within a classroom when collaborative strategies and protocols are implemented. Although the good news is that with a little patience and embracing the mindset of "less is more," this shift can absolutely occur and will be well worth it. With that good news in mind, there is much we can do to enhance collaborative strategies with the EdTech tools we have at our disposal. Ultimately, with the helpful integration of EdTech tools, we can create interactive and collaborative tasks within digital and in-person spaces.

To begin this chapter, we will discuss what the research has to say regarding student collaboration. Questions will be answered surrounding the benefits of student collaboration, how to cultivate collaborative groups where cognitive load is minimal, how we can use the knowledge-building framework to our advantage, and obstacles teachers need to prepare for before deploying collaborative student strategies and activities. Finally, our research focus for the chapter will end with a discussion of powerful collaborative instructional strategies such as collaborative concept mapping, think, pair, and share, jigsaw, structured academic controversy (SAC), Socratic seminars, and gallery walks.

With the research lens in place relating to student collaboration and its accompanying strategies, this chapter's EdTech integration vignettes will focus on integrating these strategies with mainstream EdTech tools to increase student collaboration. The goal will be to show how student collaboration strategies can span classroom settings, whether students are working virtually or in a physical classroom space. In most modern classrooms and work environments, this juggling of learning and activity in digital and in-person spaces is the norm. Therefore, our instruction must be tailored toward providing students opportunities to collaborate with their peers in-person and virtually, as 21st century jobs and industry success largely depend on this form of collaboration.

THE RESEARCH AND STRATEGIES—STUDENT COLLABORATION

Collaboration is a concept grounded in the idea that it is a "coordinated, synchronous activity that is the result of a continued attempt to construct and maintain a shared conception of a problem" (Roschelle & Teasley, 1995, p. 70). Essentially, collaboration is an activity conducted by more than one person working on a shared problem that they are trying to solve. Within classroom settings, the goal of collaboration is to help motivate and encourage students to work together to apply the skills and content they are learning in their class to answer questions to problems posed by their teacher and create content as a work product showing their collaborative problem solving (Colbeck, Campbell, & Bjorklund, 2000). Across classrooms that are in-person and digital, collaboration can look like students interacting on a physical or digital whiteboard, discussion board, a back-channel or breakout room, a document, social media, or any form of illustrative content creation application. Therefore, when speaking of collaboration, it spans an immense spectrum of activities as well as digital and physical spaces. Student actions in these spaces involve speaking, writing, listening, and creating, all in an effort toward solving a shared challenge.

With student collaboration defined, our goal is to dive further into research. First, we will explain the benefits of student collaboration and how it can result in building knowledge frameworks within classroom settings. Then, as we flow more into a conversation on collaborative instruction, we will discuss the concept of cognitive load as well as obstacles teachers face in establishing and maintaining collaborative strategies and routines. Following this information, we will explain how to facilitate student collaboration in digital and in-person classroom settings. Last, we will focus on six key collaborative-based instructional strategies teachers can deploy within any classroom setting. All of these strategies are collaborative in nature and can be integrated with a wide range of EdTech tools.

Benefits of Collaboration and Building Knowledge Frameworks

Collaboration has many benefits and proves to positively impact student learning (Chan, 2001). Research on student collaboration has shown it can motivate and encourage students to work together as they apply content and skills, which then can be used to create products (Colbeck et al., 2000). In the same light, students working in pairs or groups can help students learn from each other and produce thoughts and work products that can be more unique and innovative than if a student worked individually on the task (Alfares, 2017). Those are two major benefits of student collaboration. Collaborative learning has also been shown to elevate the development of learners; it can help create positive connections and learning networks, and it provides students with interactions that can stimulate social and intellectual improvement (Holubec, Johnson, D. W., & Johnson, R., 1998; Mastergeorgeb & Webba, 2003).

Collaboration can also help individuals construct new knowledge. The Knowledge Building Framework is a theory that outlines how organizations or groups of people who collaborate may operate and how they can create new knowledge as a result of their collaboration (Stahl, 2000). Through collaboration, we can pinpoint the needs of ourselves and others, identify the resources needed to create new knowledge, acquire or eliminate resources or processes, retrieve new knowledge through sharing, and store that knowledge through developing a work product. Ultimately, when connecting this theory to student collaboration, it establishes three elements that impact how students can work together that are beneficial to them. These three elements of the Knowledge Building Framework relate directly to student collaboration as individuals within a group setting: 1) learn how to work on authentic problems to gain understanding, 2) share collective responsibility in the problem solving, and 3) the learning results in collective knowledge building (Hmelo-Silver & Barrows, 2008). With the Knowledge Building Framework in mind, teachers can assume the role of facilitator to ask student groups open-ended and metacognitive questions and help scaffold student conversations to construct collaborative explanations and work products that aim toward solving the problem at hand (Hmelo-Silver & Barrows, 2008).

Collaborative Student Learning—Elements to Think About Before Implementation

Before implementing any form of student collaboration strategies into instruction, there are several major elements to think about. Cognitive load, student behavior, and student collaboration skills are all areas teachers must evaluate and plan their instruction around in order to make effective use of the strategies we will discuss later in the chapter. An understanding of these elements allows for the implementation of appropriate collaborative tasks for your group of students, the development of routines to help students collaborate, and the skill-building necessary for groups of students to work together effectively.

Cognitive Load

As discussed in the introduction of this book, cognitive load refers to one's working memory capacities, which are required to carry out any form of learning (Sweller, 1998). Sweller (1998) outlines how our working memory can only process so much new information at once; new information requires more mental effort resulting in a heavier load on our working memory. Ultimately, this affects learning outcomes because our working memory has only so much capacity to take on so much new information and tasks at once (Leahy & Sweller, 2008; Kirschner, P.A, Sweller, Kirschner, F, & Zambrano, 2018).

When it comes to student collaboration, there are many activities that we can incorporate to help avoid overwhelming students with too much information. Sweller (1998) recommends a number of elements that teachers need to evaluate to lessen cognitive load during collaborative tasks, such as task complexity, expertise of students in the task and content, team roles, team size, team composition, prior team experience, prior task experience, and task guidance and support.

- **Task Complexity:** Refers to the difficulty of the task. Extra steps may result in extra load. If the task is not too difficult, additional actions by team members not related to the task may result in more cognitive load. Therefore, educators must evaluate tasks based on the zone of proximal development (i.e., appropriate level of difficulty and rigor) for their students.

- **Expertise of Students:** Students who have expertise in the content and skills being taught will have less cognitive load related to the task at hand.
- **Team Roles:** Team roles make it clear who has responsibility for the various parts of the task, which will eliminate the additional cognitive load of having to divide the labor of the task and ensure individual accountability.
- **Team Size:** The more members of a team, the more interactions and transaction activities that will occur among team members, which will increase the overall cognitive load. Therefore, educators must keep teams relatively small (i.e., four or fewer students).
- **Team Composition:** A lower cognitive load will occur if students in the group have similar knowledge and skills among themselves related to the task.
- **Prior Knowledge/Prior Task Experience:** Similar to team composition, if members of the team have prior knowledge of working together or prior experience related to the task, there will be less cognitive load caused by the collaborative activities.

Teachers can strategically think about each of these elements and structure their collaborative routines and tasks accordingly, which can then be integrated into the collaborative instructional strategies outlined throughout this chapter.

Behavior Obstacles

Within group settings, a number of behavior pitfalls occur. Two competing obstacles related to student collaboration involve free riding and the competence status of one or more members of the group. Free riding refers to one or more students in the group not interacting with the other members, as well as not completing a comparable amount of the task as the rest of the group members. Conversely, competence status refers to one or more group members whose ideas are mostly accepted without much dispute from the rest of the group members. As a result, the group is dominated by these individuals, which underestimates the capacities of the other members. This can cause passivity in group members and can also result in free riding (Le, Janssen, & Wubbels, 2018). To address both of these obstacles, a number of routines and mechanisms within tasks can be assigned to student groups to alleviate these behaviors from occurring.

To mitigate these issues, teachers need to develop students' social training skills, which involve the method of organization for group activity (Blatchford, Kutnick, Baines, & Galton, 2003). Scaffolded conversations, sentence frames, modeling, and student self-reflection are all strategies that can help organize collaborative groups (Chiriac & Granström, 2012). The most important element is to ensure these strategies are consistently reinforced and conducted before, during, and after collaborative activities. To provide opportunities for all students in the group, talking cards, conversation protocols, and group facilitation from teachers can mitigate the effects of competence status. Additionally, it is important to develop groups that are heterogeneous in nature to avoid one or more students dominating the group. Teachers can strategically place students in groups, which can also help mitigate students dominating the group's ideas and work.

Collaboration Skills

Collaboration skills refer to attributes we all have when working with others. Students need these skills cultivated over time and built into the instructional design of the classroom to be effective when working with others on collaborative tasks (Larson & Miller, 2011). These skills can include communication, self-management, leadership, and problem solving (Larson & Miller, 2011). Each of these skills can be taught individually to students and scaffolded into collaborative tasks to help with skill development. For example, peer-to-peer communication can be taught in short pair shares, whole-class discussions, and communicating asynchronously on digital platforms. Self-management can be taught by providing students opportunities for self-assessment and peer assessment for non-group-based tasks. Leadership can be modeled; student class leadership roles can be given within a class setting, and group leadership can be facilitated by a teacher to one or two students within a group on a rotation basis to build opportunities to lead others. Lastly, problem-solving skills related to analytical thinking, research, assessing solutions, and generating solutions can all be taught within the fabric of a classroom throughout the duration of an educator's lessons (Lai, DiCerbo, & Foltz, 2017).

Facilitating Student Collaboration in Virtual and Digital Spaces

Within modern classrooms, we now have collaborative spaces in remote, digital, and in-person settings. Also, even within in-person settings, most of what students are working on is within a digital space (e.g., document, slideshow, video, bulletin board). Therefore, facilitating student collaboration is multi-faceted because students interact in a multitude of different ways as they collaborate on a student task.

To facilitate student collaboration within spaces that are remote and digital, there are a number of ways to create opportunities for students to communicate and create content in these settings by establishing a uniform set of EdTech tools to utilize for the class. Stephens and Roberts (2017) discuss how a useful network of EdTech tools that allow students to communicate with others within and outside of their classroom is key to successful group collaboration. Applications such as backchannel chats, messaging, and video/audio communication tools are necessary. Routines and protocols must be established using these tools within the group setting for students to use them appropriately. Also, in the same manner as communication, content creation tools can be utilized for the class and can be relatively similar for all collaborative student tasks, such as Google Workspace, Adobe, Microsoft Teams, or other software applications related to the class's content (Robert & Stephens, 2017).

Besides creating a uniform set of tools for facilitating student collaboration in virtual and digital spaces, teachers can strategically create tasks and activities that stimulate engagement. Robert and Stephens (2017) recommend creating tasks that are open-ended with no right or wrong answers, prompts that require multiple perspectives on a specific topic, and opportunities to create a wide range of authentic work products. This wide range of work products includes giving groups of students the opportunities to create artifacts and content, document the research, and have a bank of resources on how to facilitate this process. Overall, with these types of tasks in mind, students will have choice and agency, which can help enhance the students' engagement in the collaborative learning process.

Instructional Strategies that Can Facilitate Student Collaboration

As we progressed through research regarding collaborative learning and facilitation, we learned about various practices and routines to help support the strategies we integrate into our instruction. With that foundation in place, we can now focus on effective student collaboration strategies. Six major student collaboration strategies will be discussed: mapping, think, pair, and share, jigsaw, structured academic controversy (SAC), Socratic seminar, and gallery walks. Many can be implemented individually or can be combined into a collaborative task for students depending on the goal of the lesson. Also, it must be noted that concept mapping and jigsaw can be two strategies utilized in a non-collaborative function. For now, each strategy will be outlined in relation to the research.

Concept Mapping

Concept mapping occurs when students illustrate their structural knowledge visually by describing the relationships between concepts and ideas related to a topic (Jonassen & Grabowski, 1993). Concept maps can be drawn and written on a physical or digital board that is used as a learning artifact, which can be utilized for the next sequence of a task or for a future task. This strategy allows for students to work individually and then discuss within groups the application, analysis, and synthesis of ideas. Students can also begin the process of concept mapping in groups to use the ideas created by the group for an individual project or extension activity. There are multiple ways in which concept mapping can be utilized during instruction. It can be used as a way to build conceptual frameworks related to a topic of study by activating prior knowledge. In guided practice, a teacher can scaffold a concept map to encourage connection formation. During independent practice, students working in groups can collaborate to come up with ideas relating to the task or problem they are working on. Lastly, concept mapping can occur at the very end of a lesson or unit where students connect and synthesize ideas to summarize their learning. In terms of feedback during concept mapping, a teacher can provide annotated comments or illustrative or verbal feedback on the concept map, which can help facilitate conversation and the emergence of connections.

Think, Pair, and Share

Think, pair, and share is a cooperative learning strategy that gives students a scaffolded approach to student collaboration and interaction (Hamden, 2017; Kwok & Lau, 2015). To illustrate, students first are given a prompt, image, or problem to analyze. Think time is provided for students to then digest the content given to them. After a set period of think-time, often consisting of thirty seconds to a minute, is given to process information, students are then provided with the opportunity to write down their thoughts. Then, students are given the opportunity to share with a partner. Students will share their thoughts and listen to their partner's response. Following this interaction, students are prompted to add their collaborative thoughts to their initial response to form a new response. Lastly, a teacher asks two to three pairs of students to share their responses with the whole class. Additionally, teachers can summarize pair responses or provide opportunities for various pairs to share to help propel the conversation forward and sequence into the next part of the lesson. Overall, the benefits of think, pair, and share enable students to work individually as well as cooperatively. It is a strategy that optimizes student participation by providing scaffolded steps and routines for students to work collaboratively together. Finally, it allows students to synthesize information and build upon the ideas of others throughout the sequence of the strategy (Hamden, 2017).

Jigsaw

Jigsaw is a cooperative learning strategy where each member of the group needs to complete a part of the task in order for the group to complete the entire assigned task. In an effort to meet the learning objective for the lesson, students tackle the content and learning in chunks and segments (Fry, Ketteridge, & Marshall, 2008). In practice, jigsaw can take place in-person, virtually, or in a blended learning setting. With the help of EdTech tools, students can see the progress of their team members as it is made, which allows students to communicate and collaborate with each other more effectively. The main purpose of a jigsaw activity is to create opportunities for students to take on the responsibility of the learning as well as to teach others in their group (Doymus, 2008). Student learning is maximized when responsibility is provided and assumed (Aronson, Stephen, Sikes, Blaney, & Snapp, 1978).

Structured Academic Controversy and Socratic Seminar

Structured Academic Controversy (SAC) and Socratic seminar are both cooperative learning strategies that allow students the opportunity to collaborate and dialogue with each other. SAC is a strategy that can be employed by a teacher as a way to promote intellectual inquiry in a number of ways so students have the ability to navigate controversial issues outside of the classroom setting (Johnson, Johnson, & Smith, 2000). Students are tasked to build arguments based on evidence and formatting persuasive positions in addition to being able to challenge the position of others. Through this process, students work on synthesizing and integrating evidence, which can be done individually or in a team setting (Freedman-Herreid, 2005). In the beginning of the process, SAC encourages teachers to provide opportunities for students to review, analyze, and internalize the content; teachers should provide students with materials that can include arguments, supporting documents to the positions, and polarizing positions on controversial issues (D'Eon & Proctor, 2001). Once students review the material individually or in groups, according to D'Eon and Proctors (2001), there is a five-step process where groups present arguments in the form of dialogue. This five-step process is outlined as follows:

1. Group 1 presents their arguments in favor of the issue at hand.
2. Group 2 presents their arguments against.
3. Group 1 presents their arguments against.
4. Group 2 presents their arguments in favor.
5. The group members from both opposing groups must then work together to find a compromise.

Throughout this experience, a teacher acts as the main facilitator. Their main goal as facilitator is to ensure the process goes smoothly, encourages divergent thought and thinking, and asks open-ended questions to help students elaborate on their thoughts and views so they can deepen their thinking and learning (Han & Yi, 2009; Zainuddin & Moore, 2003).

Similar to SAC, the Socratic seminar is a form of instructional dialogue that is facilitated by a teacher using questions that may have been pre-selected with front-loaded content. Socratic seminar is a strong strategy to implement in collaborative settings because it provides opportunities for students to analyze questions, which has been shown to have a positive impact on student learning (Hattie & Timpereley, 2007). Alder (1984) spells out five major steps of a Socratic seminar:

1. Deconstructing a text, picture, film, or diagram, which will be the primary focus of the seminar.
2. Formulating and asking questions about the content. Questions can be posed by a teacher or by a student to the entire class. Then time is given to allow students to evaluate the questions and gather evidence.
3. Within a group setting, students verbally engage with each other by presenting arguments, counter-arguments, and evidence, asking additional questions, and cooperating to find answers.
4. As the conversation progresses, students take notes and analyze the ideas and evidence presented by their classmates.
5. Over time, as more students speak, dialogue is evaluated and students reflect and set goals to move forward in their studies.

With each step in place, the role of a teacher is to be the facilitator by asking open-ended questions and promoting cooperative conversation. Additionally, a teacher should only facilitate the conversation and never give answers to any of the questions posed. In this role, teachers must help rectify thoughts and bridge gaps in the conversation, but also provide opportunities for all students to participate and be a part of the conversation.

Both SAC and Socratic seminars aim to have students work together to search for better understanding. Although with this said, the goal is not to always result in group consensus. Rather, when implementing each strategy in your classroom, it's the goal of a teacher to encourage diverse idea creation and enhance thinking throughout the dialogue. Using seminars as forums to promote dialogue, research has shown evidence for improved language and critical thinking skills, as well as an effect on a student's ability to self-reflect and evaluate (Billings & Fitzgerald, 2002; Orellana, 2010; Pihlgren, 2008).

Gallery Walk

Gallery walk is a strategy that can be incorporated into any classroom that focuses on providing students with the opportunity to examine and evaluate the work of their peers. Similar to a gallery walk in an art gallery, students can physically or virtually get out of their seats to provide feedback to their peers, synthesize ideas by providing comments on their classmates' work, work toward building a better work product, and allow students to practice their public speaking skills as they communicate and collaborate with their classmates (Cheng, 2006). A gallery walk can be implemented as an icebreaker, summative assessment, or placed at the end of the independent practice portion of a lesson. One important practice to incorporate while implementing the gallery walk is to deploy self-assessment and assessment rubrics before and after the activity. As a result, students will have clarity and feedback toward the task related to the gallery walk and will engage in self-reflection throughout (Cheng, 2006; Kord Ali Gurk & Mall-Amiri, 2016). Overall, the gallery walk can be easily completed during a single lesson or after an extended project-based learning unit. It is a flexible strategy that can be utilized to help students dialogue, provide feedback, communicate, and collaborate to boost their learning.

INSTRUCTIONAL STRATEGY INTEGRATION WITH EDTECH TOOLS TO AMPLIFY LEARNING: STUDENT COLLABORATIVE LEARNING

Humans are wired to be social creatures, and if you ask any social theorist to outline the way in which individuals interact with the world and understand how to function within it, they will include elements of collaborative communication. Every communicative act is made up of three parts: the sender, the message, and the recipient. In an effort to enhance our students' understanding of the world, we should be providing ample opportunity for each student to converse with their peers and make meaning of the content in a collaborative manner; each student should be given a chance to participate as the sender of information, the crafter of the message, and the receiver of insight. We can provide these experiences by integrating collaborative discussion opportunities throughout our class. With a foundational background in place relating to the research on collaborative student learning and collaborative instructional strategies, it is time to focus on specific collaborative classroom activities. We will be exemplifying step-by-step processes as to how to integrate EdTech into effective collaborative strategies in order to promote student learning within any setting. The following instructional strategies will be outlined:

1. Concept Mapping
2. Think, Pair, and Share
3. Jigsaw

4. Structured Academic Controversy
5. Last Word
6. Socratic Seminar
7. Gallery Walk

As you progress through the remainder of the chapter, evaluate how you can use the research discussed earlier to optimize how you will effectively implement these strategies with the EdTech tools you have available.

Collaborative Strategies In Practice

You will now see these collaborative strategies implemented and integrated with EdTech. As you read, visualize how they will look in your classroom with your students. Then, think about how they can be adapted to meet your classroom and student needs. Ultimately, pick one to three of these strategies to start and then go from there. Let's look at how we can increase our students' collaboration opportunities.

Concept Mapping

Finding ways to connect prior knowledge to new skills, concepts and information is the backbone of any new teaching. Rookie and seasoned teachers alike begin lesson planning time by processing the best ways to help their students create schemas, both cognitively and physically, to aid in comprehension. Concept mapping can do just that. While students can work independently to create a concept map of new and existing knowledge, technology makes it easier for students to collaborate on a map, as well. Concept maps are perfect to use at any time in the learning process— during the brainstorming phase, in the middle of the project, or at the end as a way to summarize learning. Let's look at three different EdTech tools to use at these three different times in a lesson/unit. It's important to note that there are many digital tools available to use for concept mapping, and the three resources highlighted can also be used interchangeably throughout learning.

Jamboard, a digital interactive whiteboard, is perfect for connecting to prior knowledge at the beginning of a lesson. The teacher can set up the Jamboard with an equal amount of frames as there are a number of groups. It can be a blank frame for students to answer questions (via digital sticky notes), or the teacher can set the background as an image to have an unmovable graphic organizer. Students can work in small groups, adding ideas to their specific frames, but also have the benefit of seeing what other groups are thinking. The teacher, in turn, only has to access one link to view the entire class's thought processes. See Table 3.1 for directions on how to set the background as a graphic organizer:

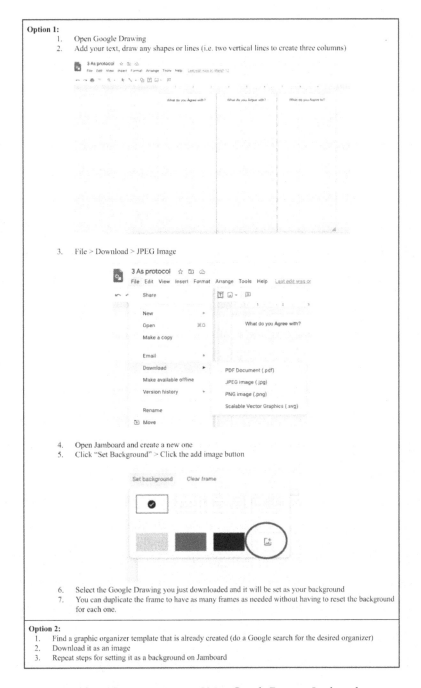

Table 3.1 Concept Mapping Using Google Draw or Jamboard

A favorite tool to use throughout a lesson is Padlet. The teacher can create one Padlet and share it with the class to have a whole-group collaborative space. Alternatively, each small group can create a Padlet and share that link with the teacher. It becomes a place to curate resources, record video and/or audio, jot down notes, link documents, and respond to each other's posts and questions. It becomes an interactive digital poster of sorts, which is built throughout the lesson/unit.

While Padlet can also be used to show learning at the end of an activity, there are also great concept mapping tools available to use within Google Slides and Power-Point. Slidesgo.com offers free templates for Google Slides and Microsoft Power-Point and even offers those specific to concept mapping (i.e., https://slidesgo. com/theme/concept-map-infographics). Collaborative groups can download one of these templates in the preferred platform and build a multimedia presentation together to demonstrate learning at the end of the lesson/unit.

Concept mapping is a strategy that can and should be employed in every grade and subject area. It is just a matter of finding the right resources and establishing clear group norms like heterogeneous grouping, groups smaller than four, each student having a specific role within the group, and establishing routines during collaborative tasks for collaboration to be successful. An example of group norms for elementary students include: Be Respectful, Be Fair, Treat Everyone Kindly, Everyone Does Their Part, and Complete the Task. Asking the class to help you further define each norm ensures clarity and ownership. Norms in secondary class-rooms should be established as a class and employed in group settings. The basis is similar to those shared for elementary students.

Think, Pair, & Share

The process of utilizing think, pair, share in the classroom was clearly outlined in the research section of this chapter. Here, we are going to look at how to apply it in a virtual or blended setting. If the class is being held synchronously, the process is much the same as using it face-to-face in the physical classroom. The teacher will pose the prompt or question and allow thought time to process. Then, the students get time to write down their ideas. The teacher then assigns pairs to breakout rooms where they will discuss their thoughts with each other. It is important that clear norms have already been established prior to this activity and that the teacher has given a designated time limit for conversation. Norms should be simple and concise: 1. Listen attentively and respectfully, 2. Share thoughtfully, 3. Discuss collaboratively. After they each discuss their responses, the pair creates a joint response to share with the entire class. At this time, the teacher brings everyone back together, and the students share verbally, in the chat, on a discussion post in the LMS, or on a Padlet.

If the virtual class is being conducted asynchronously, the teacher would most likely utilize the LMS. In an assignment post, the teacher would pre-assign pairs and post the prompt/question. Those partners could have options on various ways to share their responses— private Padlets, Flipgrids, a collaborative Microsoft Word or Google Document, and video calls would all work. They craft the joint response before posting in the designated location. The teacher could have a class Padlet or

Flipgrid set up for the "share" portion of the exercise. Both platforms also allow for comments from the entire class.

Jigsaw

There are so many great ways to utilize the jigsaw strategy to foster collaboration. When introducing a new topic, a teacher may assign different members of the group different resources to explore (videos, podcasts, articles, et cetera) and then share with their groups the key findings to collaboratively build background knowledge. In this case, a space to verbally collaborate, whether in a physical classroom or a virtual breakout room, is key. If students are working asynchronously in a remote environment, giving them a space such as Flipgrid to share their findings and comment on each other's would be an effective alternative.

While jigsawing for content knowledge is an efficient way for students to collaborate around a new topic, they can also jigsaw a final product demonstrating learning over a period of time. An example from an elementary classroom is an animal research project. Each group studies a different animal, and each student within that group researches a specific element of that animal (habitat, diet, physical features, et cetera) and then adds what they learn to a collaborative space. Padlet, Google Slides, Microsoft PowerPoint, and Adobe Express are all top-choice EdTech tools for a final research project. Giving each group an authentic audience to share their finished project adds a level of engagement that is not always there when the audience is solely the teacher.

Structured Academic Controversy

In an effort to move beyond your basic pro/con, "one side wins, the other loses" approach to discussion, structured academic controversy activities encourage students to formulate perspectives on an arguable topic and then give them the space to not only understand the opposing viewpoint, but also synthesize the information presented by their counterpart; this employs active listening skills as well as thoughtful research, focused discussion, and clear articulation of ideas. This method of discussion encourages a collaborative understanding of a concept from a variety of perspectives. Students need not only be able to argue only one side of a topic, but must understand the power that exists in working together, remaining open-minded, and coming to a collective understanding on a topic in an effort toward progressive thinking.

The first step in this process is to pose the controversial topic in question form and break your students up into teams of four. From there, each team is assigned a "side" of the topic and is tasked with researching texts/videos/et cetera that are grounded in facts/statistics; you really want to encourage your students to focus on the logos rather than the ethos or pathos of their research. Once the teams have researched, then the first group shares their insight to group B. While sharing, group B is tasked with listening actively to understand and taking notes. From there, Group B has the opportunity to share their understanding of Group A's argument by restating the different points made. Group B can also take the time to ask clarifying questions. Group A then can respond by answering the questions posed. After this, the sides switch and follow the same process and procedures. Once both teams have carried out the presenting and listening process, they then confer with their teammates and evaluate the other team's arguments; specifically, they should look for the strongest and weakest arguments made by the opposing team. Finally, the teams synthesize the information presented and work toward finding a consensus.

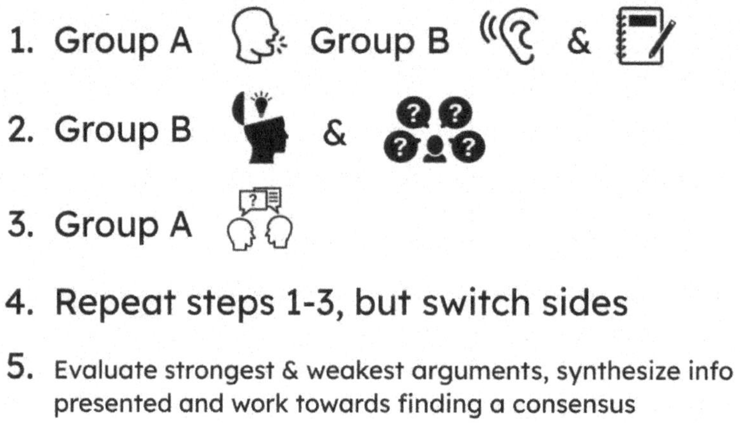

1. Group A 🗣 Group B 👂 & 📝

2. Group B 💡 & ❓❓❓❓

3. Group A 🗣🗣

4. **Repeat steps 1-3, but switch sides**

5. Evaluate strongest & weakest arguments, synthesize info presented and work towards finding a consensus

Figure 3.1 SAC in Action

Structured Academic Controversy
Note-Taking Guide

What is the controversial question we are evaluating?

Background Knowledge: What do we already know about the concept?

What are some key terms we could investigate to effectively research this topic?

My team's position:	Opposing team's position:
Main points to argue:	Opposing team's key points:
Clarifying Questions for Opposing Team	
Strongest argument	Weakest Argument
Consensus or Common Ground met?	

Figure 3.2 Notetaking Document for SAC

While this experience is more easily implemented in a face-to-face setting, it doesn't automatically disallow it to work in a digital setting as well. A great EdTech tool that can enhance this experience digitally is a resource called Parlay (http://parlayideas.com). Parlay is a discussion-based platform that allows students to interact virtually and in-person. There are built-in feedback tools that allow the teacher to provide real-time direction and encourage a structured debate/discussion.

How to create an account in Parlay
1. Navigate to parlayideas.com
2. Create an account
3. Select Teacher for user type
4. Click on "New Class" to create first course
5. Enter Course Name and Section Number for new class
6. Sign-in with SSO (Google or Microsoft)

How to set-up a new discussion Round Table in Parlay
1. Login with your SSO (Google or Microsoft)
2. Choose Class you want to create a new roundtable in
3. Select New Roundtable
4. Decide whether you want it to be ONLINE (Student-paced) or LIVE (Instructor-paced)
5. Decide if you want to choose a teacher-created roundtable from the Parlay Universe (library) or create your own
6. Develop Roundtable using easy to follow guidelines or choose from Parlay Library
7. Invite Students to participate by sharing the invite link (invite button found in upper right corner) to your LMS (Options: Copy Link, Google Classroom, Microsoft Teams)

*Note: In the ONLINE roundtables, students are assigned anonymous names to reinforce anonymity and allow them to feel more confident about not being judged. They can also submit their response and are able to add comments on their peer's responses; Parlay provides sentence premade sentence starters to get students started with peer feedback.

Table 3.2 How-to to Use Parlay for Structured Debate and Discussion

Figure 3.3 A QR Code of an Online Roundtable Dashboard Example

https://bit.ly/33FigureIWB

Last Word

In an effort to hear every team member's voice and reinforce the idea of varying perspectives, the "Last Word" activity provides an opportunity for each student in a team to share insight from an article, image, film, et cetera, and reinforces active listening and collaborative meaning-making.

1. Get into groups of 4 (max)
2. Number off 1-4
3. Designate one person to re-read _____. As they read, pinpoint one area that you would like to discuss due to it being interesting/ weird/ you connect/ etc.
4. After reading, person #1 will read the passage they wanted to discuss, but that is it. They don't say anything. Everyone else listens intently.
5. Person #2 says a few words about the passage
6. Person #3 says a few words about the passage
7. Person #4 says a few words about the passage
8. Finally, person #1 expresses why they chose the passage
9. Start the process over with person #2, etc.

Figure 3.4 Instructions for the Last Word Activity

A great resource to bring this collaborative discussion activity from one that functions in a traditional classroom setting to one that works virtually is to app smash Google Slides with Mote. A teacher can link the resource being discussed on a Google Slide and then provide an area where each student is allotted space to add an audio recording using the Mote Extension. After listening, students can reflect on the perspectives offered and evaluate next steps for exploring the topic at hand.

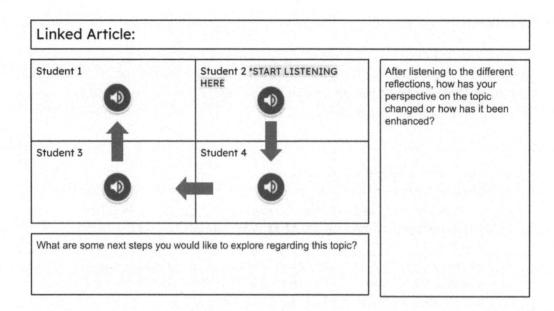

Figure 3.5 Google Slides App-Smashed with Mote for Last Word Activity

In an effort to personalize the experience even further, students can add an image to their Mote voice note placeholder, so it can go from a purple speaker to their picture or Bitmoji, or an image of choice. To change the icon, all they have to do is right-click on the purple Mote speaker, navigate to "replace image," and select a new image from their computer or Google Drive.

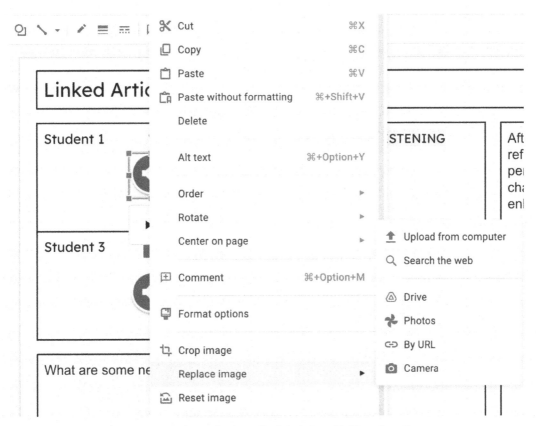

Figure 3.6 Personalizing the Last Word Activity with Bitmojis or Images

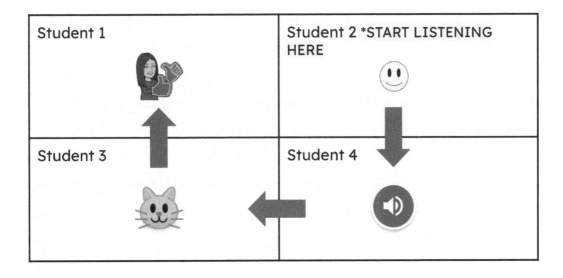

Socratic Seminar

As mentioned before, Socratic seminars are all about active learning as individuals aim to explore and evaluate deep and complex ideas in a collaborative manner through the use of questioning. Socrates believed that exploring and thinking for oneself was much more valuable than just being provided the right answer. In this activity, students are able to analyze and question a text/image/film, et cetera, and then pose those questions to their peers in an effort toward collaborative understanding. It is impossible to construct meaning in this activity without relying on the perspectives and insights of your peers. In fact, much of the purpose of this activity is for students to build off of their peers' responses rather than simply assert their own positions.

Before beginning the experience, it is important to start by outlining the difference between dialogue versus debate because the goal of this experience is to converse about a topic to establish understanding and meaning, not to assert a position, and for there to be a conclusion or winner at the end.

Dialogue is...	Debate is...
Collaborative	Oppositional
About understanding	About proving others wrong
Listening for deeper meaning	Listening for flaws
Re-evaluating assumptions	Defending assumptions
Keeping an open-mind	Close-minded
About temporarily suspending beliefs	About defending beliefs
Searching for strength & validity in all ideas	Searching for weaknesses in ideas
About respecting all participants	About belittling or demeaning others
Exploring different possibilities	Having one right answer
Open-ended	Demands a conclusion

Figure 3.7 Dialogue vs. Debate

To begin the actual process, the teacher should provide students with a text, article, and image that encourages inquiry and deep thinking. The text should be somewhat short and leave room to ask open-ended questions. To encourage think-time prior to the activity for students to process information, an educator should provide an article the night before that students can evaluate independently and come to class the next day with questions they are interested in posing. When an educator first uses this activity in class, they might want to create some questions as well that they can pose to the group if the participants bring questions that do not quite generate deep enough thought to carry a conversation. It would be useful to provide students with a digital note-taking sheet so they can write their questions down and pull specific quotes to reinforce their perspectives. Take, for example, if you were reading the book *1984* by George Orwell and wanted to discuss various ideas presented in Part Two of the novel. Students can evaluate each chapter, record their questions, and pull quotes that support their ideas or ones they felt were integral, important, or relevant to the chapter.

1984 Part 2, Chs. 3-8
Socratic Seminar

Tomorrow you will participate in a socratic seminar. In preparation for that, please complete the following chart:

Part 2 CHAPTER	QUESTION For each chapter, please generate a question that you would like to ask your peers. This question should be open-ended and created to generate conversation. If you are struggling, ask a question about the content in the chapter, that relates back to a big idea/ theme	QUOTE For each chapter, pull a quote that you think is worth investigating OR supports your question.
3		

Figure 3.8 Socratic Seminar Question and Quote Chart in Preparation for the Seminar

In an effort to ensure students are actively listening to their peers, we would encourage educators to arrange their classroom desks into a circle-type pattern, so students have to look at each other and maintain eye contact while responding. It enhances the focus while the experience develops. If an educator has a large group and cannot fit all students in a circle, or if they are teaching simultaneously (they have learners in class and ones online), they can use the platform Backchannelchat.com to encourage participation from both groups. If the group in class is too large, you can assign half the class to sit in the circle and engage with each other by verbally speaking, while the other half signs into a backchannel chat and discusses that way. Backchannel allows participants to like specific chats by clicking the thumbs-up icon. If you have students simultaneously joining the conversation, they can add to the discussion while individuals in class are sharing; you can assign a few students to act as liaisons between the virtual students and the in-person learners; their task would be to share out the perspective being offered by the virtual learners and giving a space to the voices who cannot be present in person. Additionally, this platform allows educators to view the transcript on the web after the Backchannel chat is over.

After the seminar, it is important that students think about the concepts discussed and reflect on the experience. Some questions you can ask students at the end of the experience are:

- How has your understanding matured or changed through the discussion?
- What was a key learning you will take away from this discussion?

Once these questions are asked, provide an opportunity for them to reflect, summarize, and pose questions to others in the classroom related to the discussion. This will help stimulate the conversation beyond the classroom. Additionally, it will help students reflect and practice metacognition skills to evaluate how far they have come as a result of the discussion.

Gallery Walk

In addition to producing a product related to the content in the classroom, another important skill to teach students is how to provide feedback and engage with their peers in a way that affords each learner some constructive criticism on how to move forward and enhance their product. The gallery walk is an interactive experience that gives each student the opportunity to share their perspective regarding the topic being presented. The gallery walk can be used after reading a story to discuss ideas and insights gathered while reading, as an anticipatory activity to determine where the students' background knowledge lies, as an opportunity to examine historical documents and images, for solving a multi-step equation, as an idea generator, or even after finishing a science lab to dialogue about findings.

Traditionally, gallery walks are done live and in-person, and students are given the chance to walk around the classroom with pen/pencil in hand and/or sticky notes that they then use to add comments to an individual's or group's project/product; however, in effort to be able to support digital spaces as well, a live digital whiteboard serves the same purpose. Padlet is an easy EdTech tool to support the sharing of a product with the intention of receiving peer feedback.

Imagine a physical education classroom is doing a unit on Fitness Planning, and each team is responsible for creating a collaborative infographic on one area of a certain lifestyle factor that would impact one facet of physical, social/emotional, and mental health. Teams create their infographics and then are guided on how to upload that graphic to a teacher-created Padlet. Students could then be instructed to view each of the infographics and are asked to provide feedback/comments/questions about the resource.

Additionally, if a classroom is all virtual and is collaboratively trying to make meaning of vocabulary terms as a pre-activity before starting a unit, they can use Padlet (www.padlet.com) as a starting space. Imagine your students are attempting to define the terms "Language, Gender, Culture" before starting a unit in an English course that evaluates different texts regarding the aforementioned topics. In an effort to come to a collective understanding, the teacher can ask students to define what each word IS and IS NOT. The beautiful thing about Padlet is that students can link images, gifs, videos, audio, drawings, webpages, et cetera, in an effort to answer the prompt. To mimic the Gallery walk idea, a teacher should move the learners through all the different stages.

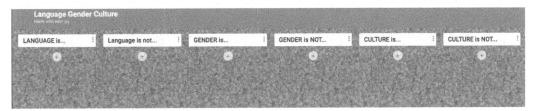

Figure 3.8 Gallery Walk Using Padlet

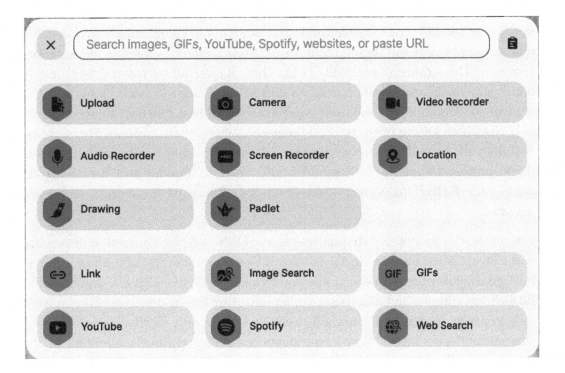

It is important to note, in an effort to make this activity collaborative, a teacher needs to give students the opportunity to provide feedback or comments on their peers' ideas after the initial defining process. Additionally, it is essential to provide the students a chance to collaboratively synthesize the information presented. For example, after students provide their definitions of what Language, Gender, and Culture "is" and "is not," a teacher can ask students to get into teams (in person or in breakout rooms), review the shares, and collaboratively define the three words using the responses on the feedback. After the groups have had a space to come up with a definition in their own words, they can share out to the rest of the class, or add it to a collaborative Google Slide or Jamboard that could then be the guiding focus throughout the unit. In this type of activity, you want to choose words that are controversial or abstract in an effort to have students stretch themselves on their path toward a definition.

CONCLUSION—STUDENT COLLABORATION WITHIN CLASSROOMS WITHOUT BOUNDARIES

In a world that is ever-more interconnected, building collaboration skills within classroom settings is essential. Beyond building collaboration skills, presenting opportunities for students to collaborate builds relationships and helps broaden the ideas and work products they create. With EdTech infused into the instructional strategies discussed in this chapter, teachers have a multitude of opportunities to develop tasks and activities for students to collaborate and create new and innovative work products that can be shared with their school, local community, and world.

Within the last few years, opportunities for students to communicate and collaborate across physical and digital mediums and spaces have become more and more common. The strategies outlined within this chapter allow for collaboration to occur anywhere and at any time. Additionally, it allows teachers to facilitate student collaboration by establishing a framework of best practices to use in whatever classroom setting they may find themselves instructing students. This foundation then allows us to incorporate research-based strategies like concept mapping, think, pair, and share, jigsawing, SAC, and Socratic seminar and then integrate them with EdTech tools that foster students' ability to collaborate and learn together.

Ultimately, the goal of this chapter was to establish a strong foundation of practice and instructional strategies to facilitate and elevate student collaboration in physical and digital spaces. We encourage you to take one or two of these strategies and EdTech integrations and incorporate them into your lesson design when you want to encourage student collaboration. Keep it simple and slowly incorporate the strategy and integration. With some patience, modeling, and scaffolding of the strategy and integration, students will collaborate in new and impactful ways in your classroom.

CONTINUING THE CONVERSATION—AGREE, ARGUE, & INSPIRED

Directions: After reading Chapter Three, what do you agree with, argue with, and what inspired you? Share your thoughts with your PLN with the hashtag #InstructWithoutBoundaries.

Agree

Argue

Inspired

CHAPTER 4
INQUIRY AND CRITICAL THINKING STRATEGIES AMPLIFIED BY TECHNOLOGY

There is no doubt that, more than ever before, students can see and experience real-world problems and experiences that society takes witness to due to their instant access to the internet; take, for example, the Mars Rover– the world was able to witness every moment in as the rover made its way to the surface of Mars all due to live-streaming capabilities. Individuals around the world can access real-time primary source videos simply with the click of a button; no longer are the happenings on the other side of the world a mystery or somebody else's problem to be solved. In the same light, the world is changing very quickly, which means our students will have to be able to understand and adapt to a variety of circumstances. Many, if not all, of our students will likely have to rework their skill toolbelt multiple times throughout the course of their lives due to the jobs that become available and because the nature of work will continue to flex and change. Thus, our classrooms must mirror this ever-changing landscape so that we can teach our students to build critical thinking skills through inquiry and investigation and promote the reality of what it means to be a lifelong learner in an effort to survive and thrive. In all likelihood, students will have many questions to solve and the tools needed to do so; however, they will need the thinking and investigative skills to put them in the position to creatively solve those problems with said tools.

What do critical thinking and inquiry look like within the classroom setting? The goal is to give our students problems that not only help them comprehend information, but to also apply, synthesize, and evaluate that information to solve problems. When thinking about inquiry, it relates to investigating a phenomenon we see in our everyday world through a procedural process to uncover conclusions. Throughout this process, we must have critical thinking skills to derive these conclusions from our investigation. Critical thinking skills are required during student inquiry so that students can identify and solve problems. Along the way, teachers act as the lead and scaffold the investigation to varying degrees. Over time, the goal is for students to become more independent and to think critically and problem-solve without the full support of teachers throughout the lesson or unit of study.

There is an assortment of challenges teachers and schools face in creating inquiry-based instructional opportunities for students to build critical thinking skills. For example, traditionally speaking, not everyone has thought that inquiry-based instruction can be utilized for all contents and skills taught in school. Historically, the perception has been that inquiry was geared more toward teaching science. Another example includes the perception that inquiry-based instruction requires the entire lesson to be inquiry-based. Similarly, in a traditional classroom, teachers give students the questions and/or topics to research and explore. Students are rarely taught how to construct their own guiding questions. While having a framework to deploy inquiry-based strategies is advantageous, inquiry-based instructional strategies can be utilized in isolation and at the beginning, middle, and end of the lesson. Therefore, each and every lesson can have an inquiry-based instructional strategy to advance student critical thinking.

As we progress into the chapter, research will first be outlined on critical thinking, such as the required skills as well as the underlying facets of Bloom's Taxonomy and its role in the critical thinking process. Additionally, we will connect many critical thinking skills to metacognition as this particular critical thinking skill helps us adapt to an ever-changing world. Then, research on inquiry will be introduced, followed by the Teaching and Learning Inquiry Framework (TLIF), which will guide how inquiry and critical thinking strategies will be discussed in this chapter so they can be implemented seamlessly into any lesson. The instructional strategies provided in this chapter relate to the five-step sequence outlined by the TLIF. Nine research-based instructional strategies will be integrated with EdTech tools and discussed later in this chapter. Through the chapter's vignettes, you will be able to see how we can take students on an investigative journey within any classroom setting. Our goal is to harness strategies and EdTech to create the framework for students to not only think critically but also to use those skills to solve problems in their local communities as well as see how they can be part of the solution to solve global problems affecting us all.

THE RESEARCH AND STRATEGIES—INQUIRY AND CRITICAL THINKING

Our journey with our research begins by discussing higher order thinking and Bloom's Taxonomy. The goal is to then outline critical thinking skills we can build within the classroom. By pinpointing those specific skills, we can use the research to illustrate how inquiry can be the pathway toward not only developing critical thinking skills but to applying them to solve problems. This will lead to seeing how the TLIF is a strong mechanism to deliver instructional strategies within any classroom setting that can facilitate inquiry-based learning to harness critical thinking skills. Last, our focus will be on discussing the research-based instructional strategies that can be built into the TLIF. In total, nine instructional strategies will be outlined to benefit your instruction and student learning.

Higher Order Thinking Skills

Let's begin by breaking down what higher-order thinking skills entail. Zohar, Weinberger, and Tamir (1994) outline how students' higher-order thinking can be built and developed by creating learning tasks and activities that can boost thinking to the next level. Over the course of these activities, students first build comprehension, which is pivotal as it is necessary to achieve in order for students to then move onto higher-order thinking taxonomies like application, analysis, synthesis, and evaluative tasks (King, Goodson, & Rohani, 2011). Before diving into each of these higher-order thinking skills, we will first see how they can be sequenced and built upon through our lessons and instructional sequences in our classrooms.

Bloom's Taxonomy

To further see how this sequence of higher-order thinking works to illustrate cognitive development, let's dive into Bloom's Taxonomy. Essentially, Bloom's Taxonomy illustrates how cognitive development involves the development of intellectual skills that are divided among domains that build upon each other, with each level requiring more critical thinking skills. Bloom's Taxonomy trajectory of cognitive domains includes knowledge, comprehension, application, synthesis, evaluation, and creation (Forehand, 2010). To achieve the various levels and to move up in the taxonomy, it requires students to have cognition skills such as recall and recognition. These skills allow students to understand facts, patterns, and concepts that build cognitive ability and higher-order thinking skills during the learning process (Forehand, 2010).

Moving up in Bloom's Taxonomy requires advancing thinking skills. For the first three levels of the taxonomy, recall and recognition are required for students to obtain knowledge and comprehension as well as apply what they have learned

(Clark, 2010). Then, achieving the top three levels of the taxonomy requires the higher-order thinking skills of application, synthesis, evaluation, and creation (Forehand, 2010; Yahya, Toukal, & Osman, 2012). However, for these top three levels of the taxonomy, we must go beyond recall and recognition. Students must be able to comprehend the knowledge they have acquired to move into the upper echelons of Bloom's Taxonomy. As a result, we must curate opportunities for students to achieve these various levels of higher thinking.

Furthermore, within our tech-infused classrooms, activities in modern classrooms that meet each of the levels of Bloom's Taxonomy involve an assortment of options. In these classrooms, students can conduct learning that includes highlighting, journaling, searching for key terms, and tagging/bookmarking as ways to begin comprehending and understanding information presented. Next, for higher-order thinking skills such as application, students can calculate numbers using online calculators, edit and make comments on a writing document, graph lines using a calculator, or develop charts and tables on Microsoft Excel or Google Sheets, and uploading various work samples from one place to the other. For the upper range of higher-order thinking skills such as analyzing, evaluating, and creating, activities to demonstrate these skills include mind mapping, surveying, linking, grading, testing, moderating, blogging, and podcasting.

As outlined above, there are a variety of activities and tasks that align directly with Bloom's Taxonomy. But, we want to dig deeper into critical thinking to pinpoint skills that make up higher-level forms of thinking to formulate our instruction around. Thus, to further understand critical thinking, we will break down higher-order critical thinking skills such as comparing/contrasting, inferring, concept mapping and creating associations, problem-solving, and reasoning that all relate to each level of Bloom's Taxonomy. Ultimately, by breaking down each of these skills, we can develop tasks and activities that activate these skills to harness, explore, and practice with them. In the next portion of the research section of this chapter, our goal will be to break down critical thinking skills and how they can be activated and cultivated in our instruction.

Critical Thinking Skills

To achieve the thinking skills to apply, synthesize, and evaluate, we must design activities and tasks that build these skills by having students problem solve, reason, compare/contrast, infer, and develop concept maps to make associations among various ideas. The goal here is to describe the critical thinking skills and then outline the types of tasks and activities that can be utilized to harness the skills within the classroom setting. Additionally, a short discussion will be provided on the teacher's role in facilitating that specific thinking skill. By providing this explanation of critical thinking skills and examples of how they can be cultivated, it will set us up to discuss how inquiry can be utilized as a mechanism to scaffold these critical thinking skills within our instruction.

First, we will define problem-solving skills and activities that help cultivate these skills. Mohd et al. (2016) describe problem-solving as opportunities for students to take a variety of different pieces of information related to a procedure as well as a concept to then put it together to address and solve a problem. A teacher's role is to act as a guide to navigate the students through the problem by planning and supporting them throughout the process. What this looks like is to teach students how to detect, monitor, test, and evaluate the process of how the problem can be solved (Jerome, Lee, & Ting, 2017). An example of an activity that allows students to problem solve involves reviewing multiple texts and asking students to complete a SOAPStone graphic organizer (i.e., identify the speaker, occasion/context, audience, purpose, subject, and tone) to then answer a writing prompt, which will require students to evaluate and synthesize information to answer. Students first use recognition to comprehend the various texts. However, without writing down or articulating all of the information about each text, students may not be able to synthesize information among them to answer the writing prompt. Throughout the process, a teacher may model where and what students may need to complete the SOAPStone in addition to providing feedback during the writing process to ensure students are following the prompt, providing evidence to support their claim, and synthesizing the information they have curated appropriately with their own analysis. Thus, as seen in this activity, students are engaged in the process of identifying information and patterns to solve the problem.

Following problem-solving, a critical thinking skill like comparing and contrasting various problems, texts, code, visuals, and multimedia is essential to navigating the world we live in today. Comparing and contrasting requires students to determine the similarities and differences in the concepts or procedures they are shown in class to analyze. It can be implemented by asking students questions that may relate to the overall big picture or related to their prior knowledge (Chidozie, Yusri, Muhammad Sukri, & Wilfredo, 2014). As a result of the compare/contrast activity, students may be able to use their prior knowledge and new knowledge they have acquired to connect the information together to develop new conclusions. A teacher's role in facilitating compare/contrast critical thinking can occur by asking open, closed, and analysis questions as well as using the Socratic method to ask questions leading students closer to distinguishing patterns. Additionally, besides questioning students, teachers can facilitate how students record the comparisons and contrasts. They can provide visuals and graphic organizers to help students organize their thoughts. An activity illustrating compare and contrast in the classroom can occur when a teacher poses two types of math problems. Then, beneath the two math problems could be a Venn diagram, which breaks down the comparisons and contrasts students could make regarding the math problems given. Supports for students can be given to frontload content beforehand to help build prior knowledge as well as for the teacher to help students solve each problem before the comparisons and contrasts are made. Besides math, this same type of instructional sequence can be utilized for any form of content and can be employed for any grade level of students.

Reasoning as a critical thinking skill occurs when we apply logic to develop conclusions from new or existing information we are given. Reasoning as a critical thinking skill can be implemented within a classroom when teachers collect student feedback, which requires students to draw on their prior knowledge of concepts and processes to elaborate and decipher meaning (Margana & Widyantoro, 2017). A teacher can facilitate reasoning as a critical thinking skill by eliciting whole class feedback on a writing sample where they can provide a series of bullet points to review. The teacher can then model on a draft where to find those areas of feedback and how to make corrections associated with the feedback. Following the modeling, students then go into their own draft to make revisions and edits based on the feedback. During this time, the teacher can question students related to the task (i.e., the feedback) with the goal of gradually releasing responsibility and allowing students to operate more independently as they progress through the revision activity. Students reason as they progress through the feedback as they must take in the feedback their teacher has given them to then apply it to their draft by identifying where revisions may be needed to improve the draft.

Inferring requires students to develop a conclusion from a set of facts or pieces of evidence. Within the classroom setting, a teacher can provide opportunities for students to develop their ability to infer by scaffolding multiple materials, text, procedures, and multimedia to then provide the students outlets to synthesize and evaluate the information and develop conclusions. An example of this can be when evaluating two different short stories that have similar themes. Students can read both stories and then draw connections on how various characters and events of the stories created similar themes, which may formulate deeper conclusions about the characters, plot, and the author's points of view. An anchor chart can be utilized to see how both stories go together by drawing images and producing text that represents schema that can help us make inferences to fully understand the text at a deeper level. Students then can formulate their conclusion in a journal, blog, discussion board, or podcast to deliver their conclusion not only to themselves but to others as well. Marzano (2010) outlines how strategically providing students opportunities to make inferences like shown above provides the foundation for students to evaluate and synthesize information to develop conclusions that solve problems.

Concept mapping and creating associations between concepts involves having students draw lines or logical connections between concepts and ideas (Sam & Rajan, 2013). Students have an opportunity to see their background knowledge and new information come together through visual thinking exercises like drawing or developing diagrams. Between the old background knowledge and new knowledge, associations can be written down, thus connecting each concept (Sam & Rajan, 2013). Different types of mapping include flowcharts, hierarchy maps, system maps, and spider maps. With these types of maps, we can create associations among any type of concept ranging from types of numbers, syntax, grammar, and punctuation, historical concept maps, storyboards, how earthquakes and Tsunamis occur, and much more for any skill and piece of content.

What is Inquiry? A Pathway Toward Critical Thinking

Inquiry-based instruction provides students an opportunity to take responsibility for their learning in a student-centered approach where a teacher poses questions, develops and provides varying levels of procedures and materials, and supports students as they discover information to formulate their own conclusions (Banchi & Bell, 2008). Ultimately, the goal of inquiry-based instruction is to gradually release students to openly investigate questions or phenomena to then develop conclusions supported by evidence. Traditionally, inquiry-based instruction was geared toward teaching science. However, in modern classrooms, inquiry-based instruction can be taught for any skill and content with the goal of fostering and developing critical thinking skills.

What makes inquiry a strong instructional model to implement within classrooms? Its premise is based on the idea and act of metacognition. Metacognition is the act of thinking about our thinking processes, which helps foster higher-order thinking by taking active control over the thinking involved in learning (Schneider, 2001). Within the act of metacognition, we think about how to approach tasks, how we comprehend information, and monitor our comprehension. Evaluating where we are in our task completion as well as how we completed the task are also acts of metacognition (Kitot, Ahman, & Seman, 2010). When metacognition is used as a form of instruction to help facilitate learning, it has had positive effects on learning outcomes for students (Zion, Michaelsky, & Mavarech, 2005).

With metacognition as the base for inquiry-based instruction, there are a number of facets that help make inquiry an impactful form of instruction. When our inquiry-based instruction focuses on the metacognitive abilities of students, we facilitate setting goals, asking questions, monitoring performance, summarizing learning, and evaluating and seeking feedback (Farah & Ayoubi, 2020; Magno, 2010). Each of these metacognitive abilities connect directly with the critical thinking skills of reasoning, problem-solving, inferring, and making associations among concepts. Therefore, inquiry-based instruction is a pathway toward critical thinking, and it has been deemed an effective form of instruction that has resulted in greater instructional outcomes than other forms of instruction, such as direct instruction (Furtak, Seidel, Iverson, & Briggs, 2012).

Teaching and Learning Inquiry Framework and Deploying Instructional Strategies to Create Inquiry-Based Learning Opportunities

To deliver a lesson or sequence of lessons that are inquiry-based, we can utilize the Teaching and Learning Inquiry Framework (TLIF) to integrate instructional strategies that help cultivate and develop critical thinking skills. This instructional design framework was developed by Molebash et al. (2019) by evaluating and synthesizing the overlap among the Common Core State Standards, Next Generation Science Standards, and the College, Career, and Civics Framework as well as the Project-Based Learning (PBL) model, Universal Design for Learning model (UDL), Inquiry Design model, and Gradual Release model. The TLIF encompasses facets and themes from each model and sets standards because it is broken down into six stages where there is a progression of knowledge and an increasing level of critical thinking skills as the lesson progresses (Molebash et al., 2019). Additionally, the TLIF has core inquiry practices and key content-building facets that require students to think, read, write, and speak by providing evidence in their responses and student work creations.

In regard to its structural components, the TLIF has six major components that can be sequenced within an instructional sequence in a lesson. As illustrated in Table 4.1, the TLIF components include: stage and engage, ask and pose, plan and monitor, search and gather, analyze and create, and communicate and apply. A short illustration of each component of the TLIF will be outlined, in addition to highlighting a number of instructional strategies that can be utilized for each stage of the framework.

Name of Component in TLIF Framework	Instructional Strategies
Stage & Engage	The 3C's Questions and Students Choose the Audience
Ask & Pose	Four Corners and Student Developed Questions
Plan & Monitor	Concept Mapping and Story Maps
Search & Gather	WebQuests/Digital Scavenger Hunts and Student Generated Surveys
Analyze & Create	Metacognition and Reflection
Communicate & Apply	Authentic Audience

Table 4.1 The TLIF Components and Strategies

Stage and Engage

Stage and engage provides students with a series of engagement strategies to activate prior knowledge related to relevant topics. Many of these instructional strategies that can be considered engagement strategies can be experimental activities such as the 3C questions, choose your own audience, escape rooms, open-ended research questions, and quick writes with a wide range of prompts ranging from those that ask students to predict, ask questions, or take a stance (Molebash et al., 2019).

The 3C's Questions. To begin any activity, a series of questions can be provided to students to help activate prior knowledge and build upon previously formed conceptual frameworks that can be derived from our students' long-term memory. The questions all relate to student curiosity, concerns, and what they may want to create. Ultimately, these three questions help set the tone of the lesson by creating engaging opportunities for students to think about what they are curious and concerned about while contemplating what they may eventually be able to create at the end of the lesson or unit. This strategy is used to set the stage for the lesson to engage our students in active deep thinking to then begin to project how they will navigate the lesson presented to them based on what they know so far.

Students Choose the Audience. One strategy to set and engage students to begin an inquiry-based lesson or project is to provide the choice to let students choose to whom they will present their findings once they have reached a conclusion. They can choose to share their findings with their classmates or a larger community through a presentation, discussion board, social media, blog, or podcast. There are many options that give students higher levels of self-efficacy because their learning is more self-regulated when choice is given to learners (Zeiser, Scholz, & Cirks, 2018).

Ask and Pose

After the initial stage has been set, teachers can then deepen students' inquiry with continued engagement throughout the lesson by asking and posing questions. A set of open-ended questions are posed by the teacher, and this set of questions drives what students research and explore throughout the duration of the lesson or unit. The questioning and support given throughout this portion of the lesson can be structured, guided, or open inquiry. All are varying levels of the spectrum for teacher support and modeling throughout the lesson. On one end of the spectrum, a teacher leads the students through the lesson by providing all of the materials, procedures, and models the entire way through. In the middle, with guided inquiry, the teacher gives students a problem to investigate along with the materials. Students then devise their own methodologies to solve the problem. Last, there is open inquiry, where students are given open-ended questions, and they must solve the task at hand with little support. There are a number of strategies to ask and pose questions to students, which include four corners, student-developed questions, the Socratic method during direct instruction, Socratic seminars, and debates. The goal of each of these strategies is to provide a stage for deep thought in structured or unstructured environments to facilitate inquiry.

Four Corners. The Four Corners (4C's) strategy provides an opportunity for students to show their position on a question as well as take a stand on their opinion (Kagan, 1989). This strategy provides the opportunity for all students to participate, whether in-person or digitally (i.e., in breakout rooms or by draggable pieces on an interactive slide) as a warm-up task or as a closure activity. It requires students to elicit an argument when they move to each corner if called upon. The question given can be an overarching question or a number of specific questions related to the content and skills being taught. Overall, the purpose of this strategy is to stage and engage students in inquiry-based learning so it can help facilitate critical thinking as well as provide students an opportunity to participate in inquiry as a new lesson begins (Marzano, Pickering & Pollock, 2001).

Student-Developed Questions. When teachers provide students the opportunity to develop questions related to the overarching question, it gives them the ability to utilize higher cognitive levels, which is an important facet of problem-solving (Pizzini & Sherpardson, 1991). Students can develop questions beginning with the *what* and then move toward *how* and *why* as they further inquire and discuss the topic with their classmates and teacher. The types of questions align directly with the various levels of Bloom's Taxonomy. For example, questions relating to *what* aligns with the knowledge and comprehension levels of taxonomy while *how* and *why*-based questions align with the *analyze* and *evaluate* levels of the taxonomy. Over time, throughout the lesson, students may be able to answer these questions as they plan and monitor their approach as well as formulate their conclusions relating to the overarching questions and objectives of the lesson. Questions can also be developed not only during the ask and pose portion of the lesson. Questions can also be created during the plan and monitor, search and gather, analyze, and communicate portions of the lesson as new questions may arise or previous questions may have to be refined based on findings made.

Plan and Monitor

During this portion of the lesson, a teacher introduces skills, procedures, and concepts. Students spend this time reviewing or developing procedures. Additionally, students set up a game plan for solving the overarching questions posed by their teacher. Strategies to help students complete this step are developing questions through concept mapping, summarizing instructions through writing, story maps, and prediction. All of these strategies are geared toward helping students plan and monitor their next steps so they can answer the lesson's overarching question(s).

Concept Mapping & Story Maps. Concept and story mapping is the process of when students illustrate the procedures and the plan of action they will take to describe the relationships between concepts and ideas related to the topic of study and the questions being asked (Jonassen & Grabowski, 1993). Students can look at a set of procedures or materials and develop a plan of action through a visualization. This can be done digitally or in print, which then provides students a guided scaffold of how they may solve a specific problem or answer an overarching question. Flowcharts, mind maps, and storyboards outlining the steps provide the visualizations and associations required to conduct sophisticated tasks that require higher levels of thinking.

Search and Gather

During this stage, students take their plan of action and test it. At this point, students explore, explain, and then elaborate. By exploring, students are testing their hypothesis and then observing what happens and collecting data to make predictions. Through this exploration phase, students can begin constructing explanations relating to the topic, materials, and procedures they are working with. After exploring, students formulate their explanations based on their observations, analysis, or data they have collected. Lastly, students elaborate on their findings by forming new predictions and questions. During this phase, they may also try alternative procedures or pathways if they did not find what they may have been looking for during their first go-through of the procedure. During this last phase of search and gather, students may compare what they have found with personal experiences and other acceptable explanations while assessing their own understanding of the conclusions they formulated. Strategies to help facilitate search and gather include WebQuests and digital scavenger hunts, collecting data from an experiment using a survey they have developed, and compiling multiple pieces of evidence from a text.

WebQuest and Digital Scavenger Hunts. WebQuests and digital scavenger hunts require students to follow a set of directions and procedures to gather evidence to then solve a problem or create a product that highlights findings. Both strategies involve a teacher selecting a topic and then interlocking text, photos, videos, websites, and podcasts to guide students through a teacher-designed trajectory where students find information and categorize over the course of the lesson or unit, which then can be utilized to answer an overarching prompt (Pak, 2015). Throughout each stage, there can be a set of tasks with structured or unguided support in the student's search for resources (Akhand, 2015). Overall, the use of WebQuests and scavenger hunts helps build reading and math skills as they require students to develop higher-order thinking skills over the course of the strategies' deployment (Stetter & Hughes, 2017; Yenmez, Özpinar, & Gökçe, 2017).

Student-Generated Surveys. When students build their own surveys, it provides them with the opportunity to collect data related to the particular phenomena they are observing or measuring. Whether it's a survey measuring student attitudes or perceptions, or a survey that helps measure how many times the egg did not break after being moved off a ledge, there are a plethora of different avenues students can take when developing a survey. Teachers can provide surveys in some cases, but students will have to deploy them during the inquiry process. The goal of student-generated surveys and their deployment is for students to formulate ways to collect data to then analyze to come up with conclusions, which requires higher-level thinking skills to be built and practiced during these processes.

Analyze and Create

Once students complete the task or activity relating to putting forth their plan to test a specific question or set of questions relating to the phenomena they are studying, it's time for students to complete higher-level thinking analysis. To analyze data and ideas that may formulate conclusions, a teacher can scaffold how students analyze the information they were able to gather. For example, a teacher may provide a template for students to summarize, create talking points, or synthesize pieces of information. A graphic organizer and a tutorial on how to manipulate the information they have collected will help students. In math or a science lab, which could be a screencast that then segues into an activity where students determine whether the problem or data they've collected relates to a specific pattern or solution. In teaching a story, a teacher can use the graphic organizer students have filled out to then turn it into a written response. Another example of how a teacher can facilitate students to analyze their information is through metacognition. By having students reflect on the activity or set of tasks they were asked to complete, students can determine through metacognition and reflection whether certain patterns and themes appeared throughout the lesson. Once this has been completed, students can articulate their reflections through writing, recorded audio, a live presentation, or video. Strategies to help facilitate analysis and creation include metacognition and reflection, scaffolded tutorials and graphic organizers, and personalized content creation choice boards. Overall, our goal is to have our students think critically about the information they have collected to then turn it into something more to be able to share it with others after deep thought.

Metacognition and Reflection. Metacognition and reflection are not only strategies to be used at the end of a lesson, but can be utilized at any time during a lesson. Metacognition and reflection help students plan, generate and revise their thought processes, summarize, and set short and long-term goals. Essentially, metacognition is defined as a series of monitoring one's own understanding, which consists of assessing knowledge or beliefs about what factors or variables interact in ways that may affect the outcome of one's thinking (Flavell, 1976). Therefore, for any skill or content taught in classrooms, opportunities can be presented to students at any time to self-assess their knowledge or beliefs. Metacognition and reflection can be deployed through a survey, sketchnote/drawing activity, mindmap, a fillable graphic organizer, or writing exercise (Molebash et al., 2019). The goal of metacognition is to provide students an opportunity to describe what they are learning and how they are solving the problem at hand, which requires high levels of critical thinking (Hacker, 1998).

Communicate and Apply

After students run through the inquiry-based sequence, students are given a range of opportunities to share their conclusions and act on what they have learned. Students have their work products created. Now it's time to give them a forum to share what they have learned with a relevant audience in an environment that may resemble life job settings. Audience members may include classmates, parents, the school, social media, or professionals within the workforce. Also, within the scope of communicating and applying, we can give our students the choice of how they want to articulate their findings through a specific medium, as well as the type of audience they will want to share it with.

Authentic Audience. An authentic audience is a strategy that involves providing students the opportunity to present their findings to an audience of choice in a format of their choice. Students, at the beginning of the learning process, determine their suitable audience and the medium to articulate their conclusions. Then, once they are completed with their project or work product, they present it to the chosen audience.

Moving Forward

As demonstrated through the TLIF, inquiry-based instruction can incorporate many different instructional models such as PBL and UDL. Through each step of the TLIF, inquiry can be facilitated by instructional strategies. Many of the strategies can be utilized in more than one step of the TLIF; however, the goal is to show how some of the most powerful strategies can be deployed to effectively facilitate each step. Going forward, we will see how each of the instructional strategies deployed from the TLIF come alive with EdTech.

INSTRUCTIONAL STRATEGY INTEGRATION WITH EDTECH TOOLS: INQUIRY-BASED INSTRUCTION

With a foundational background in place relating to the research on inquiry-based learning and instructional strategies that help facilitate it within a lesson or unit, it is time to focus on integrating strategies with EdTech. Our goal is to illustrate the strategies and integrations to show you how to implement them within your classroom setting to amplify learning when facilitating inquiry-based learning. Additionally, we will be showing you step-by-step processes as to how to integrate EdTech to enhance critical thinking. These inquiry-based and inspired instructional strategies will help develop the skills to achieve each level of Bloom's Taxonomy. Thus, for inquiry-based learning and instruction, we will focus on instructional strategy integrations with EdTech that relates to the following strategies:

1. The 3C's Questions
2. Four Corners
3. Students Choose their Audience
4. Student Developed Questions
5. Concept Mapping and Story Maps
6. WebQuests/Digital Scavenger Hunts
7. Student-Generated Surveys
8. Metacognition and Reflection
9. Authentic Audience

As you progress through the remainder of the chapter, evaluate how you can use the research discussed earlier to optimize how you will implement these strategies with the EdTech tools you have available in your classroom and school. There are many different avenues you can take in your instruction regarding inquiry-based learning. Our goal is to help add valuable strategies that can be integrated with a wide range of EdTech tools that can be added to your teaching toolbox that will boost student learning.

Stage and Engage—The 3C's Questioning Activity

In an effort to spur critical thinking about a topic, the 3C questioning activity encourages students to reflect on some of their deepest held beliefs, thus encouraging onus and hopefully calculated thought about where they stand on a subject or what they would like to investigate further. The questions or this strategy are as follows:

- What are you **CURIOUS** about?
- What are you **CONCERNED** about?
- What do you want to **CREATE** in the world?

These questions are often used as catalysts before a student jumps full force into a project. The first question incites curiosity; it encourages students to think about what they would like to research further and it is all centered around interest, which makes it even more relevant to the student. The second question asks students to evaluate their level of awareness surrounding issues in the world that they care about. When students are not only tapping into their interests, but are taking account of what they spend time worrying about, they have a clear direction that could help align their steps throughout an investigatory process; this second question moves them to think outside of their own little world and consider how they might fit into the broader world. Finally, the last question is grounded in passing off the responsibility of exemplification of learning to the student. This final question centers around creation and their ability to make an impact on the world around them. If students are given the freedom to brainstorm how they take their curiosity and concerns and demonstrate that to the world, they will be more apt to think critically and deeply about the steps they must take toward their creation.

The 3C Questioning activity can be done synchronously or asynchronously using a tool such as Wakelet (www.wakelet.com). Wakelet is an online curation board that allows individuals to add via URL, image (from desktop, GIPHY, or Wakelet's free library), written notes, bookmarks, pdf, tweets, Flipgrid video, YouTube video, Google Drive, or One Drive. They can organize and personalize their Wakelet board in a manner that suits them, and the boards can be private, public, or unlisted. Wakelet allows for individual contribution, or it can be a collaborative effort simply with the click of a button. Additionally, if the students can add the Wakelet Chrome Extension to their school computers, as they begin their search for materials to add to their boards, they can simply click the chrome extension, and it will automatically be added, and they never have to leave the site they are using for research.

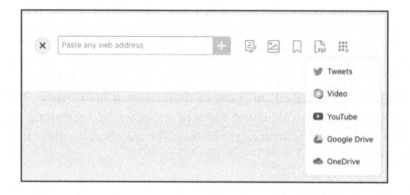

Figure 4.1 Options for Adding to your Wakelet Board

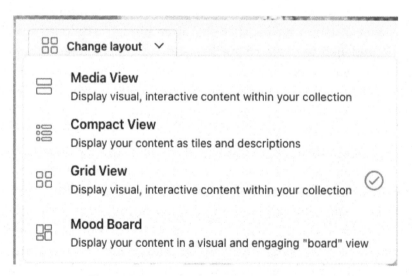

Figure 4.2 Options for Organizing Wakelet Board

When completing the 3C Questioning activity, ask students to start a board and create three categories using the "notes/text" feature. Their categories should be labeled based on the three questions listed above. After students set up the board, they can then start their research and seek out different websites, images, gifs, et cetera that support their answer to each of the questions. Students can organize and reorganize their boards as they start to brainstorm and make sense of their plan of action for moving forward in their projects. Not only is this space providing them a way to display their learning or understanding, but they are also afforded the option to do so in a visual, written, or auditory manner. Student investigation and inquiry won't be limited by one modality of expression. As they continue through the inquiry framework, Wakelet can house all their information.

Figure 4.3 QR Code of Example 3C Questioning Activity Wakelet Board

https://bit.ly/43FigureIWB

Once students set up their Wakelet board, they can invite their teacher to become a contributor by simply clicking the invite button and copying and pasting the invite link into a teacher-generated Google form which will generate a spreadsheet for each of the student's boards. Additionally, Wakelet has a feature called Wakelet Spaces; teachers can set up a space for their class or each section, and students can add their Wakelet boards. These boards then become public for all of the students to see. Students can preview their classmates' boards, and it can be a brainstorming and talking piece. The 3Cs Questioning activity could also be tweaked to be a group approach to planning if it fits the unit of study.

Stage and Engage—Student-Selected Audience

As students think about their project and what would be the best topic of interest to investigate further, they need to consider the audience they are going to be speaking to; an authentic audience is essential to effective rhetorical expression. The audience of choice will determine the ways in which they exemplify their learning. We must teach students that if they don't consider the audience, their ideas, opinions, and innovation have the capacity to be rejected. A great activity to get students thinking about their audience is the "Circle of Viewpoints" thinking routine from Harvard Graduate School of Education's Project Zero.

An effective tool that encourages methodical brainstorming is a platform called Lino.it (http://linoit.com/home). Lino.it is an online "cork" board that allows students to brainstorm using various visual features; they can add to their boards using sticky notes, images from their desktop, video URLs from YouTube or Vimeo, or document/PDF from their desktop. This platform includes a Single Sign-On through Google, or you can log in with a username/password.

Once students log in, they will create a new canvas and should be instructed to title it "Circle of Viewpoints." Teachers should then encourage students to add a sticky note that includes their focus topic for the project. From there, students need to section on three different areas of the Lino.it board and brainstorm three possible audiences (e.g., Community Board Members, their peers, their principal) to which they will be speaking. They can label these sections using sticky notes. For each section, they need to complete the following statements (image is directly from Project Zero materials):

---

1. **Brainstorm a list of different perspectives.**

2. **Choose one perspective to explore, using these sentence starters:**

   - **I am thinking of…** *the topic…* **from the viewpoint of…** *the viewpoint you have chosen*

   - **I think…** *describe the topic from your viewpoint. Be an actor–take on the character of your viewpoint*

   - **A question I have from this viewpoint is…** *ask a question from this viewpoint*

Figure 4.4 Project Zero Sentence Frames from Circle of Viewpoints Activity Materials

By the end of the exercise, students will have put themselves in the shoes of various audience members and will have a better idea of how to move forward in their project in a way that has the maximum impact.

Ask and Pose—Four Corners and Student-Developed Questions

The second step in the TLIF is *Ask and Pose*. The strength behind this framework is how it empowers students in every phase. To truly develop our students into independent critical thinkers, they must know how to identify problems, craft guiding questions, and identify possible solutions. If students aren't accustomed to developing their own questions, it's even more important for the teacher to scaffold that process through the different types of inquiry mentioned in the research portion of this chapter: structured, guided, and open. Our goal is to get our students comfortable with open inquiry, but we will likely need to start by structuring it for them.

Hyperdocs, using either Google Docs or Microsoft Word, provide a great EdTech integration for scaffolding question development. This format allows teachers to provide as much or as little guidance through this process. In structured inquiry, the teacher provides the overarching question at the top of the Hyperdoc. In the following sections of the Hyperdoc, the teacher provides the research process, the resources to explore, and the guiding questions to support the research. The teacher *could* provide some choice in how the student collects and presents the findings, but many times in a structured inquiry setting, those are also provided for the student. This method is very teacher-driven and should only be utilized if students have little to no experience with developing their own inquiry-based questions.

The next step in scaffolding this process is guided inquiry. In these situations, the teacher still provides the problem or overarching questions and some more gener-alized resources to explore, but the students have more freedom in the process. This would be a great place to introduce Webb's Depth of Knowledge to illustrate how to develop higher-level questions. Staying with Hyperdocs, the teacher provides that problem or overarching question and then leaves space for students to construct three to five questions to guide their research that will drive them back to solving the original one posed by the teacher. Depending on the age of the students, the teacher then provides resources (either specific websites or trusted databases) for the students to access for research. In guided-inquiry, the teacher should also provide some choices for how the students collect and present their solutions. This stage becomes a bit more student-directed and helps the student feel more comfortable in guiding their own inquiry process.

Finally, the open-inquiry phase is the most student-driven. In this inquiry stage, the students are given an open-ended question. Students should have various graphic organizers in their "toolboxes" to choose from to frame their research and construct guiding questions. Similarly, they should already be aware of reliable databases and/or how to conduct reliable online searches. Open-inquiry provides the most freedom for student interest, exploration, and critical thinking. They keep a focus on authentic audiences to guide their inquiry process, as well. This is where we want our students to be.

Plan and Monitor—Concept Mapping & Story Maps

After students have asked and posed their questions, they are ready to plan and monitor the inquiry process. Just like question development, this phase can and should be scaffolded as needed for student success. The first step is to create or review procedures and norms for the inquiry and exploration process. Some teachers find it helpful to create a Google Slides or PowerPoint presentation with the students as a lasting visual reminder of the procedures and norms. This can easily be linked in the LMS and added to assignments for more time efficiency once they have been established, much like a digital anchor chart.

After that, it's time for the students to establish a game plan. The first step should be for students to summarize the instructions. This serves two purposes. One, it ensures they understand the assignment. Two, summarizing is a higher-level thinking skill, so this one step helps to further develop their critical thinking. After that, concept mapping allows for in-depth thinking, visualization, and planning to occur. There are many EdTech tools that provide templates for flowcharts, mind maps, and storyboards that are free and student-friendly. Storyboard That is a popular website for creating storyboards. Students can create accounts using Google, Microsoft, or Clever accounts and can create two storyboards a week with the free version. They have access to all kinds of backgrounds, characters, and themes. The downside is that they can only choose three-cell or six-cell boards. They still offer a great option for visual thinking during the planning process and all six cells wouldn't have to be filled. Storyboarding isn't just for writing or filming. In this instance, we are using them for the inquiry process to visualize a plan. Storyboards can help students lay out what steps they need to take in order. In the beginning, teachers can provide a storyboard template with the step in each box for students to fill in. There are similar templates available in Google Drawing, as well.

Mind mapping is another strategy that helps students plan and monitor their steps throughout the inquiry process. Mindmeister is a simple and free EdTech tool. One huge benefit is that students can invite collaborators to add to their mind maps through Mindmeister. They can share it through a link or through adding emails, making it a fantastic option for collaborative projects.

Figure 4.5 QR Code to a Screencast Demoing Mindmeister

https://bit.ly/45FigureIWB

Search and Gather—WebQuest

WebQuests are a great way to get students to engage with the material before, during, and after a unit of study. When students interact with or build a WebQuest, they automatically get propelled into the role of investigator or designer. When building a WebQuest, the most important elements to consider are that there are clear parameters and that the material provided is done so using a clear and direct organizational structure. Effective WebQuests promote student independence and are well suited to the specific curriculum and personalized to meet every student's interests and needs.

The first step to creating the perfect WebQuest is to head over to Google and search (make sure you search using the topic of study plus WebQuest for more effective results) for existing WebQuests that are graciously provided by other educators and freely posted to use; if you find a WebQuest that fits your lesson/unit objective, don't forget to give credit to the original author. There is no point in recreating the wheel with such rich WebQuests already created and posted to be used; we are, in fact, #BetterTogether. However, if an educator would like to make their own WebQuest or assign a project where students develop a WebQuest, they can use Bernie Dodge's WebQuest structure as a guide.

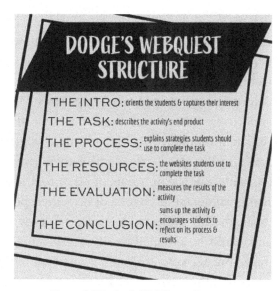

DODGE'S WEBQUEST STRUCTURE

THE INTRO: orients the students & captures their interest

THE TASK: describes the activity's end product

THE PROCESS: explains strategies students should use to complete the task

THE RESOURCES: the websites students use to complete the task

THE EVALUATION: measures the results of the activity

THE CONCLUSION: sums up the activity & encourages students to reflect on its process & results

Figure 4.6 Dodge's WebQuest Structure

Once an educator thinks through the WebQuest structure, the next step is to then determine the platform they are planning to use to design and eventually share the WebQuest. Google Sites or a hyperlinked Google Doc seem to be the easiest platforms to use to conduct a WebQuest.

1.	Navigate to sites.google.com
2.	Click + (plus sign to start a new site) or choose from the premade templates in Google Site's template gallery (**Note:** if you click "template gallery" on the top right of the screen, it will expand the template gallery and sort the templates by category)
3.	Give your site a title by double-clicking at the top of the page where it says "Your Page Title" -- This should correspond with your topic of study
4.	Change the header image by clicking on the graphic space and selecting "change image" (Note: you can upload your own image, select an image from the gallery, or search google for an image)
5.	Look to the right panel. This is where you will change the theme, add subpages, and add text, images, or files to your site; in essence, this is your toolbox
6.	Once you are done adding to the site, you will then select publish in the upper right corner where you can give the site's web address a personalized name so it is easy to find as well as set the viewing permissions.
7.	Once your site is published, you can look to the top icon bar and select the link icon to copy the site URL and share it with students on your LMS.

Table 4.2 How to Set Up a Google Site

Search and Gather—Student-Generated Surveys

A great approach in an effort to promote ownership of the searching and gathering of materials during the investigative process is to encourage students to generate their own surveys, share those surveys with their chosen audience, and then use that data to guide their expression of learning and understanding.

It is essential that students learn the power of consulting others, the representation of a diverse set of voices and experiences, and the importance of a wide range of data. In an effort to meet the aforementioned criteria, students can use tools such as Google Forms (https://docs.google.com/forms) or Survey Monkey (www.survey-monkey.com) to generate topic-related questions that will afford them clear and varied data in a time-efficient manner. Take, for example, a group of students that are creating a project where they need to identify their peers' beliefs about the school dress code. They could ask the opinions of all of their close friends, but that isn't going to give a clear or representative idea of how their peers feel because they are limited by scope. Instead, if they choose to create a survey that could be shared on a teacher's LMS and could be emailed to other educators to share with their classes, they are now receiving a greater volume of responses, thus promoting more accurate and relevant data that they can use to fuel their project.

Educators can support their students as they build, investigate, and design the survey, but it is imperative for students to spend the time contemplating the various facets of their project in accordance with their selected audience to ensure they are owning the process and growing in their critical thinking skills. In an effort to scaffold the process, an educator can provide a cheat sheet of the different types of survey questions that students can reference as they start to construct their survey.

1. CLOSED QUESTIONS: CHECKBOXES WITH A PRE-DEFINED LIST OF ANSWER OPTIONS

2. CATEGORICAL QUESTIONS: EQ: YES/NO OR MULTIPLE CHOICE

3. INTERVAL/RATIO QUESTIONS: EQ: RATING ON A SCALE OF 1 TO 10

4. LIKERT SCALE QUESTIONS: EQ: SPECTRUM OF HIGHLY SATISFIED TO HIGHLY UNSATISFIED

5. OPEN ENDED QUESTIONS: ANSWERS CAN BE SHORT OR LONG, BUT ARE SPECIFIC TO EXPERIENCE

Figure 4.7 Question Types

Analyze and Create—Metacognition and Reflection

In any inquiry process, it is essential that students evaluate the steps they have already taken and the materials/information gathered, and then take that synthesized knowledge and create something that they will eventually share with their audience. At this point in the inquiry cycle, metacognition becomes essential. Educators need to support their students as they think about their thinking and can do so with clear metacognition templates or sentence frames. The goal of metacognition is to encourage students to make sense of the information they have accumulated and acquired. Common thinking stems that will be helpful in the analysis phase are:

- I'm thinking…
- I'm wondering…
- I'm noticing…
- I think/believe that...
- This makes sense because…
- This doesn't make sense because… but I can fix it by…
- I discovered that…

To guide students through this process of metacognition, it would be helpful for them to use screen recording, screen shots, and voice over to exemplify their metacognitive reflection process. Throughout the inquiry cycle, students will have been collecting artifacts, including interviews, research materials, and graphic organizers. If a teacher wants their student's materials to be organized, the teacher can encourage them to collect the materials on a Microsoft PowerPoint or Google Slides presentation, and then record their screen while they work through the presentation. It will be important for educators to exemplify how to screenshot materials so students can add clips of their findings to the presentation in an effort to make it easier for the students to focus their reflection.

	Windows 10	Mac	Chromebook
Entire Screen	*Alt + Print Screen*	*Shift +* ⌘ *+ 3*	*Shift +* 📷
Portion of Screen	⊞ *+ Shift + S*	*Shift +* ⌘ *+ 4*	*Shift + Ctrl +* 📷

Table 4.3 How to Take a Screenshot on Various Devices

Once students have organized their learning materials into a clear presentation, using tools such as Loom (https://www.loom.com/) or Screencastify (https://www.screencastify.com/), they can share their screen and talk through the materials they found while using the aforementioned sentence frames. This activity will give educators a clear representation as to whether or not their students met their set learning goal or answered their inquiry question, but it will also act as an archive of thinking that students can reference as they begin to move forward and share with their selected audience.

Communicate and Apply

Every authentic project needs an authentic audience. Sometimes, classmates *are* the most authentic audience. When that is the case, consider having students communicate what they discovered through a gallery walk. Many times, we have students present, one-by-one in front of the entire class. Unless this time is extremely structured, most students end up tuning out after the second or third presentation. Gallery walks are one remedy to this. In a physical classroom, gallery walks can be face-to-face with various students placed around a classroom with their projects on display while other students circulate, listen, and ask questions about each project. Digitally, students can create a multimedia presentation and share links via a class Padlet or LMS discussion thread. Then, students go on a digital gallery walk through the projects to learn that way. Great EdTech tools for this would be Google Slides, PowerPoint, Sway, Adobe Express Pages and/or Adobe Express Video. All offer a great variety for creation and are easy to share.

Many times, the most authentic audience is outside of the classroom. Typically, the further removed from the classroom, the higher the level of engagement for the creator. If students are researching a problem in the community, the most relevant audience may be community members, business professionals, or school district leaders. If the audience is outside of the classroom, the method of communicating will likely be social media, class websites, or blogs. If there are very specific people who are the intended audience, consider hosting a video call with them using Microsoft Teams, Skype, Google Meet, or Zoom. Students of all ages can communicate what they found through video calls or by posting videos of their findings online. For younger students, the online presence should always be under the teacher's name and direction. Google Sites are one of the easiest methods for creating and sharing online. Students in grades two on up can handle the creation of a Google Site to pose their questions, share their progress, and their end results.

CONCLUSION—INQUIRY AND CRITICAL THINKING STRATEGIES AMPLIFIED BY TECHNOLOGY

As we have progressed through this chapter, we navigated the TLIF framework on how to integrate an inquiry-based lesson or unit as well as a set of instructional strategies to facilitate it. Along with these strategies, this chapter illustrated how to integrate a series of EdTech tools to enhance critical thinking skills. The goal of each instructional strategy and EdTech integration is to demonstrate that inquiry-based learning can take place in any classroom setting to illustrate that critical thinking can be facilitated from anywhere.

Additionally, as we close this chapter, we want to note that each of these strategies and EdTech integrations can be utilized in a wide variety of lesson plans. Not every lesson or unit has to be inquiry-based. Rather, elements of the TLIF framework and the strategies and integrations we have discussed can be used together or in isolation along with the other strategies and EdTech integrations outlined in this book. Ultimately, we want to ensure we foster critical thinking, but we can do it through a wide variety of strategies and integrations.

Moving forward, take one or two of the inquiry-based strategies and integrations to start as you begin dabbling and experimenting with them in your classroom and school. Then, over time, we recommend slowly incorporating more strategies and integrations into your instruction. Once you become familiar with a set of strategies and integrations, a full inquiry-based lesson or unit can be planned and conducted. We guarantee the implementation of the strategies and integrations discussed in this chapter will enhance your inquiry-based instruction and bolster your students' critical thinking skills.

CONTINUING THE CONVERSATION—SQUARE, CIRCLE, & TRIANGLE

Directions: After reading Chapter Four, write down your thoughts in each shape below. First, what is one thing that squared with your thinking? Second, what is one question still circling your mind? Third, what are three points you'll remember?

Share your thoughts with your PLN with the hashtag **#InstructWithoutBoundaries.**

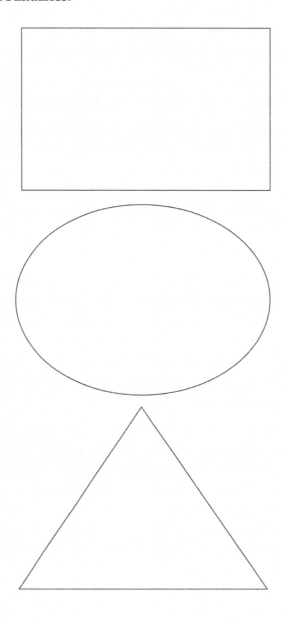

CHAPTER 5
CREATIVITY AND INNOVATION WITHIN MODERN CLASSROOMS WITHOUT BOUNDARIES

In an ever-changing world, new innovations are impacting the ways we interact with each other, and in an effort to navigate this new normal, individuals must assign creative solutions to constantly shifting problems. So, as educators, the question becomes: how can we prepare our students to not only be able to navigate our world, but also contribute to it as a partner by displaying creativity? Teaching students to be creative and innovative has always been a difficult challenge in schools; however, with new strategies and EdTech tools at our disposal, we live in a time where this is more possible than ever.

To facilitate creativity and innovation in our modern-day schools where learning is without boundaries, the Partnership for 21st-century skills (2009) developed the P21 framework, which is a set of skills that schools can teach students to navigate our ever-changing world. Schools around the world are expected to teach the learning and innovation skills of critical thinking, communication, collaboration, and creativity. In addition, along with the 4C's, students are expected to synthesize those skills within life and career domains and in information, media, and the technology they use. The challenge is synthesizing each of these facets of the P21 framework to help students be creative and innovative in school and classroom settings and have the ability to do so throughout their lives as lifelong learners as they will move between various careers and entrepreneurial ventures.

Luckily, research has provided us with several avenues, such as the Design Thinking instructional framework that addresses the aforementioned challenge. Additionally, with the help of EdTech, we can maximize our students' creativity by providing them with the choices and options to be successful in applying learned skills within the classroom and school settings, out in the community, and across social media platforms to connect and make an impact with others around the world. With the integration of technology, students can now interact with instruction and content anywhere due to the increase in connectivity.

To demonstrate how creativity and innovation can be taught in our modern classrooms without boundaries, we will first define creativity and innovation and review research on what instructional strategies boost creativity. Then, our research and strategies for the chapter will focus on the Design Thinking framework. We will illustrate the framework and connect it with Roger's (2003) Diffusion of Innovation, which focuses on the implementation of innovation within a system and how it can be harnessed and used to improve upon what was used before. Thus, concurrently, our students not only need to know how to incorporate the design thinking framework and mindsets, but also need to know how to implement their new innovations.

With this framework in place, we will focus on instructional strategies integrating Science, Technology, Engineering, Arts, Mathematics (STEAM), and Makerspaces into the Design Thinking framework to maximize student learning, creativity, and innovation. We want to quickly note that we need to think beyond creativity, innovation, and STEAM. Beyond each of these three facets, we must also know the relationships among these various elements that can interrelate within our instruction as educators and how students then can see how these three elements can fit into greater systems and organizations in our world. For example, if a student someday develops an innovative battery system to power homes, cars, and airplanes, they will also need to understand how this new invention not only affects the design of electrical systems and the battery, but also the battery and infrastructure it requires may affect the manufacturing, supply chain, and various industries. This thinking requires students to think about the big picture as well as the nuances to have their innovations be successful. We, as educators, must teach this as the world is ever-changing as well as industries. With a foundation of this thinking, they can navigate this change and have their innovations take hold that can change the world.

Furthermore, as we progress through the chapter, a discussion on how student empowerment and personalized learning will be included. Then, the chapter will focus on sharing our students' creativity and innovations with the local and global community. Conversations relating to digital portfolios, community partnerships and social media, and virtual reality will be what sum up the chapter. Overall, each of these topics and strategies will be illustrated within the chapter's vignettes as we will see the integrations in action. Ultimately, this will show how to cultivate the creativity and innovation of our students in addition to amplifying that creativity to share it with the world.

THE RESEARCH AND STRATEGIES—CREATIVITY AND INNOVATION

To begin discussing the research and instructional strategies related to creativity, innovation, and design thinking, we will first outline and define creativity and innovation. Once both creativity and innovation are defined, in addition to how to best facilitate each within modern classroom settings, the Design Thinking framework will be illustrated. Instructional strategies and instructional models such as STEAM and Makerspace that can be integrated into the Design Thinking framework will be linked and articulated. Then, the research conversation will shift toward student empowerment and personalized learning. A focus on research orchestrating scaffolded student choice, choice boards, digital portfolios, community partnerships, and enhancing voice via social media will be discussed. All of these strategies will converge and be paired with EdTech tools in the chapter vignettes, which will further elevate student creativity and innovation.

Defining Creativity and Innovation—How Do We Facilitate Them?

A plethora of research regarding creativity and innovation and facilitating them within classroom settings exists. For the purpose of this chapter and book, we will be defining creativity and innovation separately, but will then intertwine them as we believe by facilitating opportunities for students to foster and develop their creativity, we can also create opportunities for innovations to manifest from our students. After defining creativity and innovation, we will discuss how to facilitate them within our instruction.

First, we are taking Sternberg and Lubart's (1999) definition of creativity, which is "the ability to produce work that is both novel (i.e., original and unexpected) and appropriate (i.e., useful, adaptive concerning task constraints)" (p. 3). Creativity essentially is developing unique and novel ideas that can be utilized to either solve problems or illustrate new and inventive ways to articulate one's self through one or more mediums. Therefore, creativity encompasses a large breadth. As a result, Boden (2004) classifies creativity into three categories: combinational, exploratory, or transformational, which is premised on higher-level thinking skills that are involved in manifesting creative and innovative thinking. Each category illustrates how creativity is manifested. For the focus of this chapter, much of our conversation will center on transformational creativity as it aligns with the 4C's and the facets of higher-level thinking to manifest innovation.

Second, we evaluate Chatterji's (2018) definition of innovation. He asserts that education has the capacity to foster innovation and outlines the nature of innovation as a transformational process. This process includes: building, creating, testing new ideas/ products, and then improving upon what has been previously discovered, all in an effort to improve human society. Concurrently, innovation can be "fostered in education by public policies that are designed to develop, attract, and incentivize individuals who will generate new ideas" (Chatterji, 2018, p. 27). Thus, innovation is two-faceted because it requires an environment to cultivate innovation. Furthermore, by teaching creativity and creating an environment where creativity can flourish, we are fostering innovation.

How might we facilitate creativity to then help students innovate? There is an enormous amount of evidence that shows the possibility of enhancing our students' creativity through targeted education and training (Tsai, 2013). We have learned that when we focus on training and education that can affect the plasticity of our brain, we have seen how that correlates with behavioral changes (Vartanian, 2013). Furthermore, behavioral research has shown that if we build our students' skills to have a wider breadth of attention, it allows students to collect more information at the same time (Kasof, 1997; Memmert, 2007). Ultimately, if our students can work with a number of things and pieces of information at once, they may have a better chance to synthesize, connect, and build, which may increase the probability of creative thought (Martindale, 1999). Therefore, as teachers, if we can facilitate our instruction that helps expand our students' attention to multiple sources of information and optimize how we can target their attention, it may lead to better creative thinking (Takeuchi et al., 2013).

Some researchers of creativity think it is either domain-specific skills or an all-encompassing skill (Reid & Petocz, 2004). Others believe it is not domain-specific (Baer, 2010). Ultimately, what is agreed upon more is that from the instructional standpoint, we can teach either domain-specific creativity or creativity in general by the following instructional steps: 1) provide intended learning outcomes; 2) develop activities that are designed to have students meet those outcomes; and 3) build assessments that encourage creativity, which can then measure relative achievement (Marquis & Vajoczki, 2012). Through each of these steps, according to Marquis and Vajoczki (2012), opportunities present to enhance our students' creativity through our instruction.

For innovation, there are a number of instructional facets we can do along with teaching creativity to help foster the environment for our students to innovate. According to Stanford's Institute of Design (2016), teachers can focus on incorporating the following instructional models and strategies to facilitate student innovation: 1) utilize the Design Thinking framework (more on that later); 2) focus on concepts, not facts; 3) focus on student collaboration; 4) use thinking routines and EdTech tools as mediums to manifest more creative options for students; 5) reward student innovations; 6) provide opportunities for metacognition and reflection; and 7) model what innovation may look like to students.

The goal is to focus on a number of these instructional strategies and steps to facilitate creativity and innovation, but not all of them. As you may have noticed, there is a definite overlap between them. Therefore, like with any of the research-based strategies, we encourage individuals to "think less is more" and focus on a few to start and then build upon that base over time to integrate into your classroom instruction.

Skills Associated with Creativity and Innovation

The skills associated with both creativity and innovation boil down to incorporating Partnership of 21st-century skills into the Design Thinking process framework. First, we will outline the skills associated with the 4C's of 21st century learning in addition to life and career and information, media, and technology skills (as shown in Table 5.1). What this will do is create an overarching web of skills that can be built upon and then harnessed when students are put through the Design Thinking process. Ultimately, what you will see is how our students' skills in the aforementioned areas will be built, but will also facilitate creativity and innovations from our students.

As discussed earlier, the 21st century learning network developed by the Partnership of 21st-century skills consists of the 4C's, which are classified as learning and innovation skills. The 4C's are critical thinking, collaboration, communication, and creativity. Throughout this book, we have broken down each of these skills and what they all entail. However, we will spend time here summarizing these skills to illustrate the 21st-century skills framework so it can be connected to the Design Thinking process.

First, let's begin with communication and collaboration and their sub-skills. Communication consists of the sub-skill of interpersonal communication, which is

communication with others. Besides communication purposes, it is an important element of collaboration. Following this sub-skill, both collaboration and communication include writing, reading, and public speaking.

Second, we will focus on critical thinking, which we took a deep dive into in the last chapter. According to the Partnership for 21st-century skills framework, the sub-skills of critical thinking include inductive reasoning, making references, evaluation, and the interpretation of content. As discussed earlier in the book, this is much more nuanced, and a discussion on how we build higher thinking skills was outlined. Although, what is shown here is that the skills we illustrated can be summarized in these four sub-skills.

Third, we have creativity. For creativity to manifest, as discussed earlier, it requires the ability to take multiple sources of information and knowledge concurrently, which then may have a greater chance of combining, connecting, and constructing the possibility of creative thought to manifest (Martindale, 1999). Therefore, synthesis is the main sub-skill of creativity.

Fourth, we have life and career skills. Sub-skills outlined in the framework include flexibility and adaptability, initiative and self-direction, social and cross-cultural skills, and productivity and accountability (Partnership of 21st-century skills, 2009). All of these sub-skills create lifelong and resilient citizens who are required to have a fulfilling career and life in the 21st century.

Last, we have information, media, and technology skills. The sub-skills for each of these areas include information and media literacy. Underlining these sub-skills involves being able to access and evaluate information, use and manage information, analyze media, create media products, and apply technology effectively.

Altogether, the Partnership of 21st-century skills framework has outlined a set of skills and sub-skills that not only create lifelong learners able to navigate the 21st century, but also students who can manifest creativity and innovation. Therefore, the next part of the conversation will shift toward how to facilitate and develop these skills through the Design Thinking process. Additionally, we will touch on how this can be further built upon by the diffusions of innovations theory.

Partnership of 21st-Century Skills (2009) Framework		
Career and Life	**The 4Cs of Learning and Innovation**	**Information, Media, and Technology Skills**
<ul><li>Flexibility & Adaptability</li><li>Initiative & Self-Direction</li><li>Social and Cross-Culture Skills</li><li>Productivity & Accountability</li></ul>	Communication & Collaboration<ul><li>Interpersonal Communication</li><li>Public Speaking</li><li>Reading</li><li>Writing</li></ul>Creativity<ul><li>Synthesization</li></ul>Critical Thinking<ul><li>Inductive Reasoning</li><li>Making References</li><li>Evaluation</li><li>Interpretation of Content.</li></ul>	Information Literacy<ul><li>Access and Evaluate Information</li><li>Use and Manage Information</li></ul>Media Literacy<ul><li>Analyze Media</li><li>Create Media Products</li><li>Apply Technology Effectively</li></ul>

Table 5.1 Partnership of 21st-century skills (2009) Framework

Design Thinking and The Diffusion of Innovations Theory

Now, with a foundation of what creativity and innovation are, along with the skills and sub-skills that help manifest creativity and innovation, it's now time to discuss how to facilitate these skills to harbor creativity and innovation. In a two-pronged approach, students not only can build 21st-century skills through the Design Thinking process and understand the Diffusion of Innovations theory, but they can also manifest creativity to then innovate. As educators, our job is to facilitate this in our classrooms. Therefore, as we go through the Design Thinking process and the Diffusion of Innovations, we will also discuss how Makerspace, STEAM, personalized learning, and student empowerment fit into this equation.

Design Thinking

Design Thinking was first formulated by Simon (1969) and then illustrated for the design world by Rowe (1987). Then, the Stanford Institute of Design began to be one of the major advocates pushing for Design Thinking within educational settings (Bush, McCurdy, & Nichels, 2020). The goal of pushing Design Thinking into the educational sphere was to try and increase student engagement and motivation by providing a forum for students to ask "why" they are learning about a specific topic or skill. By establishing Design Thinking as a forum and systematic process to understand the "why" in what they are learning, students need to formulate and redefine solutions to the questions and problems they face, which is similar to those in the field in any professional capacity. Furthermore, a series of studies that focused on the implementation of Design Thinking found that tasks and activities associated with it produced higher levels of student achievement, motivation, engagement, and self-expression (Mehalik, Doppelt, & Schuun, 2008; Scheer, Noweski, & Meinel, 2012). Ultimately the overarching goal of Design Thinking is to help students develop 21st-century skills as well as provide relevant connections and avenues to guide students toward contributing to solving problems we face now as a society.

Design Thinking involves a five-step framework, which involves students taking a problem or question(s) to then emphasize, define, ideate, prototype, and test to see if conclusions can be formulated. The five-step framework and its implementation are key to it being successful for your students. For the purposes of this book, we are summarizing and curating Stanford's Institute of Design's steps and frameworks related to Design Thinking (Stanford Institute of Design, 2016). Therefore, we will define each of the five steps and then focus our instruction on how they play out within the classroom setting. Then, we will discuss how to further integrate STEAM and Makerspace into this framework as instruction extensions to Design Thinking.

· · ·

The five-step process of Design Thinking begins first with **"emphasize."** This is where students observe, engage, watch, and listen to phenomena or content related to the overarching questions; this step can also address the "why" of the proposed focus/task. Essentially, this can be students exploring and researching information, which frontloads students on possible routes of the Design Thinking process they may take in the future. In the classroom, this can be a set of documents students review, open-ended research, or information presented by the teacher. Then, students write down or compile their initial thoughts and reflections before they commence the next steps.

The second step of Design Thinking is **"define."** During this step, either in a scaffolded approach or in a more open approach, the focus is provided to the problem, and criteria and goals are created for evaluating ideas to begin thinking about how to tackle solving problems. Simultaneously, this is a time when terms and concepts are defined for the project ahead. Last, this is time to not only develop goals for solving the problem, but also create team-related goals to empower and inspire groups of students, individual students, or entire classes of students focused on solving the problem at hand. During this time, students can write down a list of terms and goals so they know the direction they need to go.

The third step is **"ideate,"** which means taking in a variety of ideas from the group and/or outside perspectives to undercover areas of exploration in addition to creating flexibility for innovative options that may begin formulating. During this time, solutions may begin to be presented and debated with the goal of going beyond the obvious and simple solutions to increase the potential of possible innovations. In the classroom, group discussions, Socratic seminars, and debates, along with collaborative and cooperative learning activities, allow students to ideate and determine the next steps.

Fourth, we have the **"prototype"** step. The prototype phase of the Design Thinking process is a time where ideation turns into testing possibilities of the plan, design, or prototype. During this step, we begin with the "why" of how this specific plan may or may not work as well as what it will take to manage the outcomes when each plan is implemented. Additionally, the "how" is the actual building and tinkering with the prototype, which involves identifying what future users may want in addition to what variables may arise as a result of the prototyping that may tip the project into success or failure. Within the classroom, Makerspace, the physical building of the prototype, and the development of demonstrating and showcasing the prototype occur during this time.

The fifth and final step of the Design Thinking process is the **"test"** phase. The test phase involves refinement, which relates to the prototypes that have been created, our point of view, and what users the prototype has been developed for. Additionally, it's an opportunity to show what has been created and provide experiences for users. Through the use of compare and contrast, individuals can also identify ideas for use that may have been previously held. In the classroom setting, the test phase provides opportunities for students to present what they've developed and tested. Whether through a digital portfolio, the actual prototype, or a more formal written product, students have multiple avenues to demonstrate their learning in the test phase of the Design Thinking process.

Integrating STEAM, Makerspace, and Personalized Learning into Design Thinking

Within the Design Thinking process, we can integrate the principles of STEAM, Makerspace, and personalized learning. STEAM refers to incorporating Science, Technology, Engineering, and Mathematics in a multidisciplinary approach in the classroom. Makerspace is the overarching physical, social, emotional, and digital environment where we put things together. Personalized learning gives students choice and provides a variety of opportunities and mediums for students to demonstrate and share their learning. Overall these underlying themes and environments can help strengthen the Design Thinking process because they amplify the agency in determining the kinds of things students are engaged in and making (Hughes, Morrison, Kajamaa, & Kumpulaninen, 2019). When we take concepts of STEAM and Makerspace and integrate them with Design Thinking, we must think of it as a social product because it is a complex social construction that can affect a student's perceptions and practices along with the processes of production (Dufva, 2017; Lefebvre, 1991). Throughout the innovation process, there is a creative design, manufacturing, problem-solving, and testing phase, but it involves a multidisciplinary approach because, in the real world, the problems we face can be within any discipline and are across multiple disciplines.

Integrating STEAM and Makerspace in Action

What does the integration of STEAM and Makerspace look like along with Design Thinking? Rauth, Köppen, Jobst, and Meinel (2010) outline how STEAM and Makerspace can be integrated into Design Thinking by taking the process and interconnecting it with pieces of instruction focused on human-centeredness, bias toward action, radical collaboration, building a culture of prototyping, showing, not telling, and the mindfulness of process. Knowing each of these facets is helpful because they can be framed as a mindset when integrating STEAM and Makerspace into a school and classroom. First, human-centeredness is empathy toward people and seeking feedback to create optimal designs. Having activities centered on thinking about how others feel about ideas, beliefs, or products is an important start. Second, bias toward action refers to the overarching biases we bring to the table while we create versus taking into consideration multiple perspectives of others. As creators, we tend to favor our biases unless there are opportunities to seek and understand the perspectives of others. Therefore, we develop activities to provide multiple perspectives from others to help with this. Third, radical collaboration involves being together with students with different backgrounds and enabling varied viewpoints to emerge into insights and solutions. Students come from all different backgrounds. Be intentional by having students share their background, beliefs, and viewpoints toward the problem while collaborating. Fourth, the culture of prototyping refers to taking each step of the Design Thinking process and having a prototyping mindset. In practice, this means students can always go back and revise each step. Students can make changes, and the end of the project or activity in the classroom does not mean it is over for the student. Fifth, "show don't tell" relates to students' ability to communicate their vision and work product by telling a relatable story that is visually impactful and creates experiences for the audience. Think about what a TED Talk looks like. When students are presenting and communicating their findings, make it like a TED Talk. Focus on the story and visuals of the product versus words on a slide. Last, the mindfulness of the process refers to having goals in each stage of the process and practicing metacognition. By providing students opportunities to set goals and reflect in a journal, a daily form, or a bulletin board each and every day, we help students be mindful of what they are doing and learning.

As we can see, when having each of these facets interconnected, an environment where students can cultivate creativity and innovation can emerge. Illustrated in Table 5.2, you can see how the Design Thinking process can be integrated with STEAM and Makerspace themes. Later in the chapter, we will see this in action along with EdTech integrations to further enhance this instruction and student learning.

Design Thinking Integrating STEAM and Makerspace Principles and Themes	
Design Thinking	**STEAM and Makerspace**
1. Empathize 2. Define 3. Ideate 4. Prototype 5. Test	• Human Centeredness • Bias Towards Action • Radical Collaboration • Culture of Prototyping • Show Don't Tell • Mindfulness of Process **Note:** Each above theme can be incorporated into every step of the Design Thinking process.

Table 5.2 Design Thinking Integrating STEAM and Makerspace Principles and Themes

Diffusion of Innovation—Showing Students How Innovation Fits Into STEAMs

Along with Design Thinking, we wanted to touch on Rogers's (2003) Diffusion of Innovations theory because our students need to learn how their innovations may fit into a greater system we see within the world and organizations, as well as how they can be adopted. Our students must know that innovation without having the ability to be readily adopted will not be an innovation that succeeds or is seen by many. Ultimately, Rogers (2003) describes how innovations are only impactful if someone or an organization believes the practice can be readily adopted and has a relative advantage or efficiency over what was used before. Additionally, he describes how the innovation needs to be compatible with existing models and methods and demonstrates simple ease of use. Last, he mentions that the innovation can provide a degree of experimentation and can perform and show observable results over time. To illustrate the Diffusion of Innovations in action, Figure 5.1 depicts how various groups adopt new technology over time. Furthermore, teaching students to understand the adoption of innovation is just as important as the strategies and thinking skills used to formulate innovations.

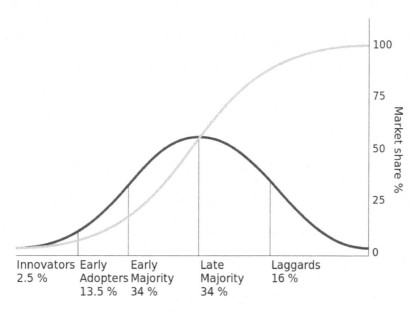

Figure 5.1 Rogers (2003) Diffusion of Innovation Describing Successive Groups Adopting New Tech

How is this illustrated and conducted within the classroom setting? At the instructional level, we must show our students conceptually as well as through illustration what systems look like relating to the content and skills we are discussing in our classrooms. We can use concept mapping, Venn diagrams, infographics, virtual reality experiences, and videos to illustrate the system. However, we must move beyond illustrating the system. Students must also know how a change to the system may affect the system. For example, a system many of us are familiar with is greenhouse gas emission from fossil fuels, which in turn, create higher concentrations of carbon dioxide in the atmosphere that traps more heat in Earth's atmosphere. Students need to understand in this example how carbon dioxide levels trap heat. As a result, students can see how new innovative technology like carbon sequestration captures emitted carbon dioxide, leading to a decrease in the effects of global warming and climate change.

Besides seeing conceptually what a system looks like, to further understand how innovations or disruptions to a system may affect the system, a number of opportunities can be provided to further teach this to students. Teachers can use research activities, group discussions, debates, and Socratic seminars to have students dive deep into how the innovations may fit into the organizational system it interrelates with, as well as how they can and may be adopted by people or societies interacting within that system (Marquis & Vajoczki, 2012). Systematic relationships are important for students to dive deeper into in order to see how future innovations can be incorporated into a system for a long-lasting positive impact.

Overall, Design Thinking helps harness and build student creativity and innovation. Then, students analyze and evaluate how that innovation may best fit into existing systems. By taking the principles of the Diffusion of Innovations theory and combining it with Design Thinking, students can then pinpoint and find advantageous ways to incorporate it into existing STEAMs people within our societies use. As a result, if our students understand Design Thinking and the Diffusion of Innovations, it can lead to students who not only can manifest innovations, but also incorporate them into our society for long-lasting impact.

Empowering Students through Student Choice, Digital Portfolios, and Community Partnerships

Through the Design Thinking process, we want to foster our students' creativity and problem-solving skills to facilitate the development of innovations. When facilitating this process within classrooms, one of our goals is to empower students, which may lead to more creativity and innovation. What does this look like in practice in classrooms without boundaries? In our current day, we can create avenues of choice as well as mechanisms for sharing our students' work with their local school community as well as globally. Thus, we will illustrate how we can develop opportunities for student choice and sharing with the world to empower students. Additionally, our classrooms now can create community partnerships locally and globally for students to connect and experience how what they are doing in their classroom relates to what they may be doing when they enter the workforce in the future.

Scaffolding Student Choice

To empower and motivate students, we can provide them with choice as they complete activities and tasks within the classroom. However, too much choice may lead to too much cognitive load. Remember, cognitive load relates to too much information being processed at once, which then limits how much we can learn at a given time (Kirschner et al., 2018). Sometimes, when student choice is given with the appropriate structure and scaffolds, students may get lost or take much longer to create a work product. Essentially, the best example is like walking into the grocery store without a list. Therefore, we must scaffold student choice to avoid this problem. For example, in an effort to ensure success on a student choice board, it is imperative that teachers include opportunities for students to build their prior knowledge and develop conceptual frameworks before they are given a choice of how to demonstrate their final work product. Additionally, students need to know how to utilize the EdTech tools and understand the expectations of each choice offered. As a result, providing examples of exemplary work samples, multimodal directions (e.g., text, audio, and/or video), a rubric, and video demonstrations on how to utilize the tools given to create that final work product affords students the necessary resources to be successful. Ultimately, by giving our students scaffolds, it does not erode opportunities for creativity or innovation. Rather, it gives students a direction and prior knowledge to use the tools to incorporate student choice to create new and innovative work products that demonstrate what they know.

Digital Portfolios and Social Media

Social media provides multiple spaces for students to share their work products with their classmates, school, and the world. Digital portfolios are excellent digital spaces where work can be uploaded and shared through social media. The goal of sharing student work through digital portfolios on social media is to facilitate peer learning and assessment (Barrett, 2003; Wenger, White, & Smith, 2009). We want students to use digital portfolios as this vehicle because they can be ongoing spaces to store student work, demonstrating their abilities and skills to see its evolution over time. Future schools, teachers, and even future employers can evaluate digital portfolios. Digital portfolios ultimately create higher levels of engagement and can demonstrate not only student work but also interaction with other students and the local and global community. They highlight the relationship among students, their work, and the community (Lawler, 2013). Additionally, through sharing and having students or the greater community comment on the work that is shared, it allows students, while developing work and digital portfolios, to improve their metacognitive skills as they receive feedback (Clark, 2009).

In practice, each student can either develop a digital portfolio at the beginning of their educational career or within a specific class. Once an activity or project has been completed, it can be uploaded as a specific page or hyperlink on the digital portfolio, which then can be shared on social media. The social media page can either be the student's individual account, the school's account, or the teacher's class account. Depending on your school and district's privacy rules regarding social media use, this will dictate whether it's okay or not for social media posts.

Community Partnerships

Teachers are centerpieces of community partnerships that can be made locally and globally (Hill & Taylor, 2004). If teachers are pragmatic in organizing these partnerships over time, designing classroom and home activities involving families, and maintaining community connections, it helps form partnerships that are long-lasting (Hill & Taylor, 2004). Now, there are a number of ways to connect with these partnerships. Whether it's coming into the classroom, field trips, digital field trips, or virtual calls with professionals and experts in the field, we can immerse our students with experiences where they have opportunities to see how their work extends beyond the classroom setting.

A variety of EdTech tools can make this all happen in modern-day classrooms. Virtual reality gives students the opportunities to participate in virtual explorations, experiences, and simulations that were previously infeasible (Wei, Dongsheng, & Chun, 2013). Also, in the VR realm, students may have opportunities to experience careers and experiences within the classroom that otherwise would not be possible, like exploring the solar system, constructing buildings, or assisting in the emergency room. Additionally, with the help of virtual video conferencing tools, students can meet with experts and have them discuss what projects they are working on and how the activities in class may connect to what they are doing, and how the world may be changing.

Ultimately, teachers and schools have a variety of different mechanisms to formulate local and global community partnerships. Teachers now have many opportunities to connect with experts in the field using social media as well as several tools such as virtual video conferencing and VR to have students experience the community, connect with experts, and simulate experiences that otherwise would not be available within the four walls of a classroom. Never before in history can teachers forge these types of partnerships and have their students experience things in the classroom that were once impossible a few years ago. Thus, take advantage of your local and global community. Connect them with your students and have them experience the world!

INSTRUCTIONAL STRATEGY INTEGRATION WITH EDTECH TOOLS: CREATIVITY AND INNOVATION

With a foundational background in place relating to the research on creativity and innovation, along with the instructional strategies that help facilitate these essential skills within a lesson or unit, it is time to focus on integrating strategies with EdTech. Our goal is to illustrate the strategies and integration to show you how to implement them within your classroom setting to amplify your students' learning by providing the instruction and classroom environment to harness student creativity and innovation. Additionally, we will be showing you step-by-step processes as to how to integrate EdTech to exemplify how creativity and innovation can not only be harnessed and built by our students but also shared with the local and global community. Ultimately, these instructional strategies spur and build innovation in addition to helping individuals develop the 21st-century skills that will help them navigate and make an impact in our ever-changing world. Therefore, for instruction relating to creativity and innovation, we will focus on instructional strategy integrations with EdTech that will relate to the following strategies:

1. Design Thinking in Action
2. Makerspace and STEAM within Design Thinking
3. Play and Prototyping
4. Choice boards
5. Genius Hour
6. Community Partnerships
7. Virtual Reality to Experience
8. Harnessing Social Media to Share and Learn

As you progress through the remainder of the chapter, evaluate how you can use the research discussed earlier to optimize how you will implement these strategies with the EdTech tools you have available in your classroom and school. There are many different avenues you can take in your instruction regarding inquiry-based learning. Thus, our goal is to help add valuable strategies that can be integrated with a wide range of EdTech tools that can be added to your teaching toolbox that will amplify student learning within classrooms without boundaries.

STRATEGY AND EDTECH INTEGRATION

As we begin seeing the research and strategies being illustrated and integrated with EdTech tools, you will see how the foundation of Design Thinking in our lessons and instruction can revolutionize what can be done in a classroom without boundaries by teachers and students. Throughout the vignettes demonstrating these strategies in action, you will see Makerspace, prototyping, choice boards, Genius Hour, community partnerships, VR, and harnessing social media to share and learn with the world. By the time you are done reading and seeing these strategies and integrations in action, you will see how student creativity, innovation, and voice can be amplified.

Design Thinking with Hands-On Learning

While students all have different learning modalities, the connections made through hands-on learning experiences benefit all learners. This is especially true when fostering creative thinking skills. STEAM, Makerspaces, and Design Thinking all provide opportunities for students of all abilities to tap into their natural creativity while also increasing their innovative thinking skills. The Design Thinking process works naturally within Makerspaces and engineering within a STEAM curriculum. After learners have identified a problem and ideated various solutions, they move to the more hands-on component of prototyping. There are various EdTech tool integrations throughout the entire process, but some specific hands-on components include design templates via Google Drawing, Canva, 3D printing, and robotics.

Prototyping Templates & Design Thinking with Makerspace

Many educators think the Design Thinking Process is too advanced for our primary-aged students. However, even our kindergarteners can build their creative muscles using the process. One example for younger learners is posing the problem of approaching cold weather. They ideate various solutions on how to prepare/dress for that weather change. Teachers can find or create templates online of simple body shapes where students can draw and color various prototypes of clothing choices. Students should have between 4-8 shapes to create and modify their ideas. This simple idea can be adapted for a variety of topics by changing the template.

For older students, the idea of designing an app to solve a problem that they have identified can be mapped out on wireframe templates. One high school health class wanted to create a new exercise app. After they conducted some research, they decided what components they wanted their app to have and monitor. Then, they

116

used a wireframe template to visually map out their prototype. This template is easy to create in Google Docs. Students can then work on their prototypes digitally, or print out the template and draw them instead.

Figure 5.2 Wireframe Templates

If your school has access to 3D printers, students can design their prototypes and print them out. There are free 3D printing design software options. Tinkercad remains a favorite for use in classroom settings. Students can choose from designs already created or design their own. The Design Thinking process can also help learners see that they don't always need to 3D print an entire model. Maybe a model is better prototyped using cardboard, Lego, or other materials with only a key piece coming from a 3D printer. The prototyping phase is an important part of determining that information.

Makerspaces become the ideal place to both prototype and test solutions. Many Makerspaces are filled with EdTech resources such as Spheros, Ozobots, and Makey Makeys, but low-tech materials are also valuable in fostering creativity and innovation. Giving students the space, resources, and guidance to create in an open environment like a Makerspace removes boundaries often associated with traditional classrooms and allows their minds to explore creative possibilities.

Hands-on learning experiences can, and should, fit into all content areas, though they seem to fit more naturally into those associated with STEAM. Science, Technology, Engineering, Art, and Math all lend themselves to inquiry, which naturally leads to the design thinking process where creative thinking flourishes. Prototyping and testing designs are at the heart of engineering.

Too often, in standards-driven curricula, there is little time for learning through play. Add to that the misconception that play means free-for-all, and that time gets even narrower. Instead, think of giving students the opportunity to explore, build, test, and refine those opportunities where they are learning through play. Learners of all ages need that freedom to create that comes naturally when we give them the space, resources, and guidance to do so.

Personalized Learning and Student Empowerment

To enhance our students' creativity and innovation, let's put them into positions that personalize their learning as well as empower them. As educators, we can put our students in the driver's seat in their own creative journeys by designing our lessons to be personalized and full of choice and opportunities for their work and voice to be amplified. To begin this process, choice boards will be discussed, followed by digital portfolios. We believe both of these can be designed into all of our lessons to create a culture where personalized student learning and empowerment are the pillars of the classroom instructional culture. Then, we will cover Genius Hour, which provides a time and place for students to tinker and choose their own learning pathways to be creative and innovative. Altogether, we believe by incorporating one or more of these three facets into your instructional design, you will see more creative and innovative work products being developed by your students as well as more buy-in to what's being taught in the classroom.

Choice Boards

As previously mentioned in our Assessment and Feedback chapter, choice boards are easy to create and can allow students to feel empowered in the exemplification of their learning. While teacher-crafted choice boards are great tools for alternative assessment, students can also flex their creative muscles and create choice boards to demonstrate their understanding of a concept. These student-generated choice boards can then be used as assessment tools.

A fun activity that can be instituted in a traditional, blended, or virtual model is a jigsaw group activity based on the students' area of expertise (Abed, Sameer, Kasim, & Othman., 2019). Take, for example, a physical education teacher doing a unit on volleyball. That educator can start the unit by reviewing the lesson objectives and academic vocabulary that students need to know in an effort to remain focused during the unit. Once the teacher has set the groundwork, they can then break students into groups and assign one area of focus to each group from the unit. From there, those student groups become the experts in their assigned area and are tasked with creating a choice board that encourages mastery of their focus area. Their choice boards should contain a balance of information (research articles, YouTube videos, websites, et cetera) provided to peers in an effort to ensure a well-rounded understanding; in addition, students should consider what product their peers will develop that exemplifies their mastery of the concept. The choice board becomes a one-stop, student-generated shop for the class to understand the different aspects of the unit.

Volleyball Unit - Areas of Focus	
Group 1	Passing (individual & partner)- Footwork & Technique
Group 2	Setting (individual & partner) - Footwork & Technique
Group 3	Hitting - Footwork & Technique
Group 4	Serving - Positions & Technique

Table 5.3 Unit Development Using Choice Boards

In an effort to encourage creativity and innovative thinking, give the basic instructions and let students determine how their choice board will look. You could include the following instructions to prompt the group thinking:

- As a group, start by mapping what you ALREADY know about your assigned topic
- Conduct research as a group to fill in the blanks and gather more information
- As a group, discuss your strengths (video, audio, drawing, painting, writing, et cetera)
- Delegate responsibilities. Each group member will be individually responsible for bringing ideas to the table as to how they will fill in their choice board
- Make sure your "assessment types" and information are varied and balanced

This approach to choice boards will encourage engagement, collaboration, creative thinking, as well as an onus over the subject. By the end of their group effort, each select group of students will become an expert in the area and can support their classmates as they work through the different choice boards. The unit is no longer teacher-driven, but rather student-driven and full of innovative thinking that has the capacity to push the limits.

The choice boards can easily be constructed using Microsoft PowerPoint/Google Slides or Microsoft Word/Google Docs. If students would prefer to complete an analog choice board, they absolutely can and then scan the document and create QR codes that can be assigned to each box that requires the use of the internet or a virtual response platform.

Digital Portfolios

As the world continues to progress toward an era where more and more interactions with the world include digital experiences, encouraging students in the creation of digital portfolios over the course of their educational career has the capacity to leave them with a working resume by the time they graduate high school and move into either college or a career. Often, students are asked to complete a digital portfolio for an assessment or grade, but when you give students the chance to collect and compile their work over the course of a longer period, they can then use that material to reflect on growth or even get a job. Additionally, students can set learning and career goals and reflect on them over the course of their educational career, thus making their reflection continuous rather than episodic. In many secondary settings, keeping a digital writing portfolio allows students to see the progression of growth in their writing skills while also giving each year's English educator the opportunity to assess where the students are in their skill level. Students can keep similar portfolios in courses that are cyclical and build on skills year to year, such as their art classes, social studies, science courses, world languages courses, et cetera. The goal of a creative digital portfolio is not for the students to be assessed on their work, but rather to task the students with the creative representation of their learning. The best digital portfolios include artifacts that are both digital and analog. (Students can scan and upload images/PDFs/et cetera, or they can scan and upload QR codes that can be scanned on the go with most devices.) Google Sites or Adobe Express Page is a great resource to build digital portfolios (as mentioned in our Assessment & Feedback chapter), but some other great resources for digital portfolio development are KudosWall (https://kudoswall.com/education.php) for younger students and bulb (https://my.bulbapp.com/student/) for older students. There is also a premium digital portfolio site called PortfolioGen (https://www.portfoliogen.com) that mimics the features of LinkedIn but for students.

KudosWall	bulb
1. Login in https://kudoswall.com/education.php 2. Click "Start Building a Portfolio for Free" 3. Sign-Up by completing the form 4. Select Account Type 5. Complete Basic Information and press register 6. Complete User Registration and add subcategories to personalize your experience 7. Activate your account by checking the email sent 8. Login to dashboard 9. Press the green button on the bottom right to add to the portfolio	1. Login to https://my.bulbapp.com/educators/ 2. Click "Sign up for Free" 3. Sign up with an SSO (Google, Microsoft, or Clever) 4. Fill out the Registration Form and select Create Account 5. Optional: Take the built-in tour to familiarize yourself with features 6. Add cover image and profile photo 7. Press Select "Create Page" and add materials to the portfolio
https://bit.ly/54FigureWallIWB	https://bit.ly/54FigureBulbIWB

Table 5.4 How to Login and Platform Dashboard

Genius Hour

The epitome of creativity and innovation is grounded in an approach that was first introduced at Google called Genius Hour. Educators quickly caught on to the practice and have implemented the practice in their own classrooms in an effort to promote creativity, ownership, and engagement. Genius Hour, aka 20% Time, aka Passion Projects, is when you give students set aside time to research and work on a project of their choosing. When you implement Genius Hour, the number 1 rule is to not limit your students by your own limitations, but rather help support them as they consider their interests, how they are going to research those interests, and how they will share their findings with the class. During Genius Hour, educators become cheerleaders and docents, celebrating and guiding students on their path toward innovation.

Genius Hour is effective for all students, but especially for those students who struggle to connect with the "traditional" method of school. Genius Hour turns students from passive learners to investigators and creators. According to an

EdSurge article by Jen Schneider, there are three basic rules to consider when implementing Genius Hour in your classroom:

1. Students must start with an essential question that cannot be answered with a simple Google search
2. Students must research their questions using reputable websites, interviews, and/or print resources
3. Students must create something. This product may be digital, physical, or service-oriented. (Schneider, 2018)

It is important to make it clear that students have the creative liberty to investigate and express themselves however they see fit, but they must follow the basic rules of the process. Initially, you might have some students stuck when you ask the question: What are you passionate about? At this point, to support students who are uncertain of what direction to head, you could use a brainstorming activity where you establish a set amount of time and ask them to quickly list their interests and explain why they are interested in their listed topic/item. You can encourage students to free-write; students who feel more comfortable brainstorming by hand can have that option; those that are more comfortable digitally can use a Google Doc. Once they have identified some interests, you can ask them to rank those interests in priority order based on when they have the most fun or feel most alive. Additionally, you can ask them to consider interests/topics that they don't yet know much about but perhaps are curious about. Encouraging curiosity usually leads to masterful creative expression.

The beauty of Genius Hour is it encourages students to push themselves outside of their comfort zone. They will need your support through periodic check-ins and when they share their final product. As a result, you should be prepared to provide them with different tools/resources that will support their expression. Additionally, you will have to provide scaffolds and build routines and norms around Genius Hour to build up to being able to implement further gradual release and independence as students become accustomed to the routines and norms that are expected during Genius Hour. Be sure to be intentional with the routines and norms and practice them over time before expecting students to become fully autonomous during Genius Hour. Some useful tools are illustrated in Figure 5.3, and they are broken down into several categories that represent the types of content that can be created during Genius Hour.

Video	Audio	Written	Image	Site/Blog
⮕ WeVideo ⮕ Screencastify ⮕ Apple iMovie ⮕ Loom ⮕ Microsoft Stream ⮕ Flipgrid	⮕ Vocaroo ⮕ Swivl's Synth ⮕ Mote ⮕ Voice Recorder	⮕ Google Docs ⮕ Microsoft Word ⮕ Apple Pages ⮕ Google Slides ⮕ One Note	⮕ Google Drawings ⮕ Canva ⮕ Adobe Express Post	⮕ Google Sites ⮕ Adobe Express Page ⮕ Wix ⮕ Blogger ⮕ WordPress

Figure 5.3 Genius Hour EdTech

Note: Genius Hour is all about creative freedom, and all it takes is an hour a week to let your students thrive and get excited about something that isn't "required" by the pacing guide. Passionate endeavors deserve to be encouraged, and Genius Hour is the first step on that path.

Community Partnerships and Social Media to Share Student Creativity and Innovation

Reading Partnerships

Establishing reading partnerships throughout a community is a great way for students to connect with people of different ages, cultures, or even countries! We no longer have to consider a community to just be what surrounds us geographically. Technology gives learners access to global communities to stretch thinking and provide new perspectives. EdTech integrations may seem obvious with the increased use of video chatting software. Reading partners can "meet" through Zoom, Teams, FaceTime, and Google Meet. They can come with a book to read to one another or with their partners. This synchronous reading time especially benefits our youngest learners, as well as those learning a second language or who have special learning needs. In other cases, reading partners can come ready to discuss a shared text and spend their time reflecting and discussing. Not only are the students increasing their reading fluency and comprehension skills, but they are also becoming better communicators and deeper thinkers in the process. The reading process becomes more innovative as the students tap into partners outside of the classroom walls.

VR/AR—Experiences of the World

Over the last few decades, and largely due to social media, the world has become a fast-moving, smaller place that affords students and educators limitless opportunities to engage globally. Students have grown accustomed to the reality of digital experiences and relationships, and because of that, their attention spans have shrunk. In an effort to make the world, ideas, and connections more accessible while meeting students where they are, education has turned to the way of Virtual Reality (VR) and Augmented Reality (AR) experiences. Educators often ask students to "imagine" a place, concept, idea, or moment in history, but using VR/AR technology, students can now go beyond imagination and immerse themselves in the experience.

Imagine an educator is teaching a Career Technical Education course, and the students are doing a lesson on Career Exploration. Using Nearpod's built-in VR function, students can visit worksites and experience what an environment might look like for a future career of choice. All an educator has to do is visit the Nearpod website, search for "Career," and then choose a variety of experiences that have been carefully curated for the purposes of career exploration. Or, say, a social studies course is studying the United States of America: each student can be assigned a state report and using Nearpod VR, they can explore their specific assigned state. Nearpod's VR feature also gives students the opportunity to study force using a roller coaster simulation or even evaluate the process of photosynthesis. The options are endless and simply require a Nearpod account. Using Nearpod, students no longer have to "imagine" what a place, career, environment, concept, or idea is like, but rather can immerse themselves in the experience. Nearpod also offers teacher-paced or student-paced so the experience can happen synchronously or asynchronously, depending on classroom needs. Additionally, you do not need special VR goggles to experience Nearpod's features.

Figure 5.4 A Preview of Nearpod VR Selection

If you do have a set of VR glasses/goggles for students to use, there is a great channel called Virtual Reality on YouTube that has curated VR 360 videos for students to explore using gear. The playlists range from gaming experiences to travel opportunities to eyewitness views of historical and current events. The opportunities for immersing students in a virtual experience are endless.

Augmented Reality, like Virtual Reality, makes ideas and concepts come alive; however, Augmented Reality (AR) allows students to see objects in the real world, while virtual reality transports students to a virtual world. A couple of highly popular AR apps used in education are MergeEDU (https://mergeedu.com/), which allows students to engage with 3D objects and simulations in the science and STEAM field, and FigmentAR (https://viromedia.com/figment), which gives students the chance to make interesting stories come alive. Neither application is free, but both offer students immersive experiences and give them the chance to creatively think about concepts that were once foreign to them.

Google Arts and Culture (https://artsandculture.google.com/project/ar) also offers FREE AR experiences simply by downloading the app on a smartphone or tablet. Using this application, students can be hands-on zoologists, astronomers, or archaeologists simply with a click of a button. Educators everywhere no longer have to be responsible for bringing artifacts to the classroom, but rather students can take control of their investigations and gain a better understanding of the world around them, and all they need is a compatible digital device.

Entrepreneurship

As schools continue to promote creative and innovative thinking, we will see more and more students embracing the power of entrepreneurship and innovation in the workforce. As educators, we need to provide experiential activities that encourage students to explore their passions and interests as well as provide them the skills necessary to thrive in a transactional world; as more and more schools realize this reality, entrepreneurship courses and units are popping up across the world of education. Students are beginning to realize the power that exists in being their own boss and the beauty of small business ownership, and educators everywhere must support them on that journey.

Educators interested in instilling an entrepreneurial spirit need not look further than Knowledge Matters's Virtual Business Simulations (https://knowledgematters.com/highschool/). Using this platform, students are able to experience a range of industry work, and educators can use the resources provided to create an interactive web-based experience.

Figure 5.5 QR Code of Knowledge Matters Virtual Business Simulations
Options

https://bit.ly/56FigureIWB

Knowledge Matters has created a unit of study for each industry that includes information, activities, and assessments, all crafted to provide students with the ultimate experience. This organization believes that knowledge isn't created by simply reading a textbook, but rather by immersing yourself in actual experiences that require the participant to make real-world, creative decisions.

To gamify the entrepreneurial experience, Cool Math Games has come up with a few games that promote the business-minded experience; on this web-based platform, students can run a Lemonade Stand (https://www.coolmathgames.com/0-lemonade-stand) or Coffee Shop (https://www.coolmathgames.com/0-coffee-shop).

Altogether, entrepreneurial activities encourage students to think innovatively and really push the limits. These types of activities cater to all backgrounds and types of students because they push the limits of what students expect from a typical school day. Creative expression is essential to this process, and the brainstorming, planning, implementation, reflection, and reiteration process is engaging and can appeal to most students in any educational environment.

How Social Media Sharing Can Build Community and Empower Students

Once students hit middle school ages, many of them are proficient in multiple social media platforms. It's typically the number one way tweens and teens communicate with each other. Being able to tap into that draw for educational purposes engages students in environments with which they are usually most comfortable. If parental restrictions are a concern, the teacher can always create a class account on one platform to use for learning purposes.

Assuming that parents and administrators see the inherent value in social media in the classroom, it becomes an invaluable tool for connecting learners, building communities, and empowering students to be creative and innovative thinkers.

Fostering creativity sometimes requires experts outside of the classroom. Social media offers an easy pathway for research and contacting experts in various fields. Typically, if an "expert" has a strong social media presence, they will welcome the opportunity to share their thoughts and knowledge with students. Similarly, it encourages students to think more creatively about what constitutes an expert. Social media platforms open the opportunity for experts to connect with students around the world. Keeping privacy and safety in mind, Instagram continues to stand the test of time with tweens and teens alike. It provides a place to share images, video, and text, and also direct communication through direct messaging. By enlarging the community, students broaden their life perspectives and can move forward in growing as creative thinkers.

CONCLUSION—CREATIVITY AND INNOVATION WITHIN MODERN CLASSROOMS WITHOUT BOUNDARIES

In modern classrooms without boundaries, there are more opportunities than ever before to empower your students to be creative and innovative. With the Design Thinking instructional model along with strategies that increase student learning, EdTech can be integrated to put our students in the driver's seat to manifest new innovations and be content creators. As the world evolves and puts the tools in our hands to be innovative and creative, our job as educators is to teach our students the skills to be creative and innovative.

We now have opportunities for our students to become entrepreneurs, see and interact with places and people that were never before accessible, dabble with new concepts and ideas, partner with their local community, and collaborate with students and experts in the field from across the globe. Additionally, we have tools available for students to create video, audio, software, text, illustrations, and inter-active worlds. Last, we can provide opportunities for our students to share all of their creations and innovations with the world through digital portfolios to house our students' work longitudinally over the course of their educational careers, along with social media to share and their creations and innovations. Digital port-folios have the capacity to empower students by giving them agency and a unique voice; these portfolios allow them to share who they are and what they value and showcase their creations. The opportunities are endless. Take a few of these strate-gies and integrations to give your students a platform to be creative and innovative while building their skill sets in those areas. Then, share with the local community and even possibly the world what your students are doing and creating, which may inspire more creativity and innovation as well as even lead to an innovation that may change our lives, the lives of our students, and people around the world!

CONTINUING THE CONVERSATION—I NOTICED, I WONDERED

Directions: After reading Chapter Five, write down several key themes you noticed. Then, write down at least three to five questions or statements that relate to your next steps of taking what you learned in this chapter and applying it to your practice and classroom. Share your thoughts with your PLN with the hashtag **#InstructWithoutBoundaries.**

I Noticed	I Wondered

CHAPTER 6
THE AGE OF FORMATIVE ASSESSMENT AND FEEDBACK

Two of the most important elements of instruction are assessment and feedback. Without each working hand in hand, we cannot gauge student learning and provide instruction to support students at the individual, group, and whole-class levels. In this digital age, formative assessment has never been easier or more effective. With the advent of modern EdTech tools, teachers have the ability to assess students and provide high-quality feedback quickly and efficiently to reach all of their students being taught in a classroom. When feedback mechanisms are embedded into each assessment, teachers can strategically provide tasks for students to do something with the feedback they have been given to extend their learning and bridge gaps in student understanding regarding a skill and concept. In one recent meta-analytic review of the literature analyzing over 225 studies on assessment and feedback, the researchers found that assessing students raises academic achievement and offering collective feedback provides a variety of benefits for learners, such as additional exposure related to memory retrieval, transfer appropriate processing (i.e., associating meaning with information that strengthens memory), and student motivation. Significant effect sizes relating to assessment (i.e., elementary school .238, middle school .597, and high school .655) and feedback (i.e., .537) were found after their analysis (Yang, Luo, Yu, Vadillo, & Shanks, 2020). Undoubtedly, assessment and feedback impact learning and must be a cornerstone in our instruction. However, we must also be clear that assessment and feedback effectiveness comes down to the quality and context of its implementation within the classroom, which is what we will articulate throughout this chapter (Wiliam, 2012).

What does assessment look like in modern classroom settings? Ultimately, assessment helps teachers determine the level of student learning in relation to the lesson's established standards-based learning objectives. In addition to using assessment as an opportunity to gauge student learning in the moment, we are also using it as a jumping-off point that will direct all subsequent lessons. With the advent of the digital and internet age in classrooms, the ways to deliver assessment and feedback have changed immensely. There are numerous EdTech tools to create assessments, as well as a vast amount of tools that create opportunities for students to demonstrate learning. Instructional practice and EdTech tools have evolved, and we now have the power to provide feedback through a variety of different mediums such as text, voice recordings, video, images/graphics, GIFs, and memes.

Often, when assessment is discussed, the idea of grades and compliance comes to light. We want to focus on the usefulness of feedback versus grades and compliance in this chapter. In essence, feedback should be what drives student learning and teacher instruction. We will share how to manifest the best research-driven strategies for feedback that can be given to students to support them in their learning as a result of formative assessment. This chapter aims to synthesize the concepts of formative assessment and feedback together with several instructional strategies that can be further amplified by EdTech tools to support student learning in an equitable manner. Additionally, we will focus on what effective feedback and assessment look like in today's classrooms.

Guided by research, we will illustrate what a variety of effective assessments look like, how they align with learning objectives and the best methods of implementation for all different types of classrooms. Additionally, factors affecting assessment will also be discussed, such as cognitive overload and how to avoid falling into the trap of using assessments to track students versus focusing on student development. To complete the research on assessment, we will discuss how formative assessment is now the most effective form of assessment and the impact it has on facilitating student learning. Following the discussion of the body of research on assessment, feedback will be defined as well as we will provide an illustration of the different types of effective feedback that can be provided by teachers to students. Feedback will also be outlined in terms of creating feedback routines that are associated with students taking action after feedback has been given by a teacher. Last, feedback will focus on student self-assessment in the form of self-reported grades as well as students' provided feedback for their teachers.

THE RESEARCH—ASSESSMENT

Assessment encompasses a broad spectrum of mechanisms that allow teachers to measure the effectiveness of their teaching to student performance in relation to specific learning objectives (Stassen, Doherty, & Poe, 2001). Why is assessment important? In a practical sense, it provides teachers and school leaders with diagnostic and longitudinal feedback. We learn about where the students' knowledge and performance base lies, what their specific needs are, and what has to be taught to support students in an effort to meet learning objectives. Additionally, the feedback students receive from an assessment can affect their motivation and provide baselines for self-evaluation on what is working for them, dissecting where they may need more help and support, and providing a direction on where they should go next.

Formative vs. Summative Assessment

There are a variety of different types of assessments that teachers can deploy to assess for evidence of student learning. First, we will begin with a formative assessment. Formative assessment is an assessment that provides a snapshot of what students know at that moment in time that the assessment was conducted (Maki, 2002). As a result of formative assessment, teachers can share results with students, and students can reflect on how they can improve. Fortunately, as we have moved into the digital age, formative assessments have become easy to administer and have become an efficient and effective way to collect student data as well as provide students with immediate feedback. Findings show that online and digital formative assessments were successful when a teacher was active in the assessment process and involved in moderating and providing student feedback during the experience and after it had been completed (Armellini & Aiyegbayo, 2010). Additionally, formative assessment is effective when it stresses major concepts, themes, and performance-based objectives versus students identifying key details through memorizing facts (i.e., multiple choice-based assessments) (Lawton, Vye, Bransford, Sanders., Richey, & French, 2012). Formative assessments accompanied by opportunities for students to self-evaluate their levels of knowledge and skills allow for students to have higher overall assessment scores (Van Gog., Sluijsmans, Joosten-ten Brinke, & Prins, 2010).

Summative Assessment

Before jumping into sub-groups of assessment, we will briefly discuss summative assessment. Summative assessment is a mechanism to assess student learning after the end of a course of student learning (i.e., unit of study, trimester, semester, school year, et cetera). Examples of summative assessments include midterms, final exams, papers, and long-term projects, which are designed to summarize student learning (Maki, 2002). One of the major downsides of summative assessment is that it does not provide many opportunities for students to reflect on what they have learned along their learning journey, as well as limits the ability to demonstrate growth in what was assessed once the assessment has taken place. In modern digitized classrooms that include the effective and timely delivery of formative assessments due to readily available EdTech tools, the need for summative assessments has been greatly reduced over the last five years. Also, with a focus on optimizing our feedback to students, we want to design our assessments to provide opportunities for intentional feedback to be given in order for students to see where discrepancies in their learning have occurred, as well as promote self-reflection and evaluation of their next steps.

Formative Assessment

Formative assessment is an evaluation of student learning within a given time frame. Its major purpose is to determine a student's level of achievement so that the teacher can provide feedback and enhance student learning during the course of a lesson (Maki, 2002). Teachers can quickly interpret student performance now with dashboards and interfaces linked directly to the assessment EdTech tools being delivered to students during instruction. As discussed later in this chapter, teachers can use formative assessment to help students "understand their strengths and weaknesses and to reflect on how they need to improve over the course of their remaining studies" by providing feedback to facilitate learning in order to improve their achievement (Maki, 2002, p. 11). Formative assessment provides opportunities to improve student learning; therefore, the focus of formative assessment is to lead students in interpreting results, reflecting on growth, and using that information to enhance their understanding.

Different Types of Assessment: Alternative Assessments

Beyond formative and summative assessment, there are different types of assessment that fall under each category. We will summarize these various types of assessment as they can all be integrated with EdTech tools to be delivered to students to enhance their learning. Following is a short outline of performance assessments, peer assessments, self-assessments, and digital portfolios.

Performance Assessments

Performance assessments provide opportunities for teachers to measure a specific skill or ability (Frey & Schmitt, 2010). Scoring of performance assessments is generally completed by a rubric that is aligned to learning objectives and success criteria. Oberg (2010) summarizes performance assessments as "one or more approaches for measuring student progress, skills, and achievement" and concludes that performance-based assessments are "the ultimate form of linking instruction with the assessment" (p. 5). Performance assessments are authentic in nature as they can put students in real-life context scenarios. This helps students contextualize the skill that was taught for a specific role and problem.

Peer Assessments

Peer assessments provide students with opportunities to collaborate and evaluate their own work and that of their peers (Brown & Knight, 1998; DiCarlo & Cooper, 2014). The goal of peer assessments is to provide "ownership of learning and focus on the process of learning as students are able to share with one another the experiences that they have undertaken" (Brown and Knight, 1998, pg. 52). Like performance-based assessments, rubrics aligned with learning objectives and success criteria can be utilized with students to conduct this self-assessment and as an evaluation of their work and their classmates. Additionally, similar to performance-based assessments, peer assessments (depending on how they are orchestrated) can provide students with real-life context problems to solve with their peers.

Self-assessments

Self-assessments give students the opportunity to reflect and practice metacognition skills to help them identify their own strengths and areas of improvement within the content and skills they are learning. Self-assessments can be a quick questionnaire form or a writing reflection. They can be used as a formative and summative assessment that goes alongside formalized teacher-based assessments as they do not have a strong correlation with student competence (Gabbard & Romanlli, 2021). Ultimately, self-assessments can be viewed by a teacher and a student as a space where dialogue relating to student learning can take place, which can help inform both parties of where the learning needs to go as the student progresses through the class.

Digital Portfolios

Digital portfolios, also known as e-portfolios, are a collection of diverse and authentic evidence of student learning drawn from a larger base of student work artifacts representing what a student has learned over time (Barrett, 2003). Digital portfolios also represent how a student has reflected and designed the learning artifacts for a presentation with fellow students, their teacher, school, parents, and the greater community (Barrett, 2003). Overall, a digital portfolio represents what learning has taken place over the course of time, which may have already been assessed by a teacher, peers of the student, and/or the student themselves. Another goal of digital portfolios is to encourage students to assume ownership of their learning through reflection and self-assessment.

Considerations to Evaluate Before Delivering Assessments to Students

Before delivering an assessment, as well as when we are conducting an assessment, there are a number of facets we must take into consideration to help increase our students' learning. There are four important topics we will summarize as they are imperative to think about when planning and administering an assessment. We will outline how to support students during assessment (ensuring we are not cognitively overloading our students), how to ensure our assessments relate to our learning objectives and success criteria, and how to create opportunities for assessment and student empowerment.

Supporting Students While Taking Assessments

To help our students with assessments, several supports can be embedded in almost every assessment to ensure assessments are accessible to a diverse set of learners. Delaney and Hata (2020) suggest the following five essential supports: reading directions aloud, providing a video outlining the assessment's directions, showing an example or model of how to solve the assessment's task, keeping the on-screen assessment uncluttered, and modeling the instructions by completing one example question together. In practice, we can do this in a few different ways—we can embed an immersive reader into assessments in addition to creating two short videos demonstrating how to complete a sample problem, as well as including a video with the assessment's directions. All of this can be uploaded to the student's LMS along with the assessment itself for students to access. Overall, supports like those mentioned by Delaney and Hata (2020) create a level of accessibility for assessments as well as provide clear and specific examples of how students can get started with it.

Cognitive Overload

Have you ever felt overwhelmed when an assessment has too many steps or too much information to multi-task? This is called cognitive overload because there's too much information to process that goes beyond our limits for processing language (Van Merriënboer, Jelsma, & Paas, 1992). Everyone has different levels of cognitive load, but there are ways to mitigate it for all our students. Therefore, when creating and delivering assessments, we must be intentional with ensuring our assessments are not too dense with information that students cannot process the information well. To help our students avoid cognitive overload, our assessments should provide visual directions. Additionally, we must create tasks that do not require much multitasking. Three is generally the number of new pieces of information we can handle simultaneously. In addition to meeting the needs of all learners, we must also include these supports to help avoid cognitive overload.

Learning Objectives and Success Criteria

Learning objectives give teachers and students a benchmark to meet in relation to what students are learning. Learning objectives are generally derived from federal or state educational standards. Success criteria are steps along the way we must take in order to meet the learning objective. Assessment comes into play with learning objectives because they are designed to measure growth in relation to the learning objective. As a result, assessments must be designed to align with our learning objectives to ensure what we are measuring for the desired outcome for our students' learning. Always begin with the standard, create your learning objectives and success criteria to meet those objectives, and then design your assessments. This methodology will keep each of these elements in alignment. We will be able to evaluate how our students are doing in relation to what they should be able to do by the time their course of study has been completed.

Assessment and Student Empowerment

Student empowerment and assessments intermix when we provide students with direction and opportunities for reflection and goal setting. After an assessment takes place, it is important to provide students opportunities to reflect and then set goals for improvement. Moeller, Theiler, and Wu (2012) found that student self-assessment and goal setting over time correlates with indicators of student achievement (i.e., test scores). Additionally, the role of self-efficacy (the belief in one's self) was shown to also increase when academic goals were present, which directly correlates with self-motivated academic achievement (Zimmerman, Bandura, & Martinez-Pons, 1992). Thus, we must provide opportunities for our students to reflect and set goals. These actions can empower our students to achieve not only academically, but also set them up for success in many facets of their life.

INSTRUCTIONAL STRATEGY INTEGRATION WITH EDTECH TOOLS TO AMPLIFY LEARNING: ASSESSMENT

Since we now have a background in the research relating to what effective assessment looks like within classroom settings, let's focus on strategies and EdTech integrations that will illustrate how this will work. For assessment, our goal will be to discuss instructional strategy integrations with EdTech that relate to the following:

1. Formative Assessments
2. Alternative Assessments
3. Success Criteria
4. Choice-Based Assessments
5. Alternatives to Writing
6. Visual/Auditory Expression

Each of these themes within the assessment domain will help elaborate on how teachers build assessments that can then be utilized as mechanisms to deliver feedback to students.

Forms of Assessment in Practice

As discussed before, many different forms of assessment will be exemplified in this upcoming section. We aim to show you several examples of assessments that can be implemented as formative and alternative assessments within any classroom setting. Depending on the instructional scenario, many of these forms of assessments can be deployed for both. In this section, co-created rubrics, choice boards, digital portfolios, alternative forms of writing, and informal interview assessments will be outlined. Remember, the goal of these assessment examples is that they can be incorporated into any type of content and grade level. Therefore, as you review

138

each type of assessment, think about how it can be incorporated into your instruction, as well as the EdTech tools you have available for your classroom.

Co-creating Rubrics

We're all familiar with traditional multiple-choice tests. These types of assessments rely heavily on basic recall and rote memorization. From those test results, teachers typically get very little insight into the active growth in critical thinking or retention of content knowledge. Fortunately, there are myriad alternative assessments that provide those insights while engaging students in higher-level thinking.

As mentioned above, assessment design should begin with established success criteria. An effective practice in lesson design involves the KUD protocol (Tomlinson & Imbeau, 2010). What do you want your students to **K**now, **U**nderstand, and be able to **D**o. When those are established for each unit, it leads to the creation of success criteria for each lesson and for the unit as a whole. Once the teacher has success criteria decided, it's time for rubric creation.

This book is about boosting student learning. As such, students need to be involved in every facet of their learning experience—this includes rubric design. Even teachers of primary-grade students can successfully involve them in creating a rubric to guide assessment.

As a class, use something like an interactive whiteboard or a good old-fashioned piece of chart paper to begin the creation. Start with sharing the success criteria with the students (in student-friendly language). Including them in brainstorming what types of products would demonstrate the mastery of these criteria. Then start determining what the various levels of mastery would look like to start filling in the rubric continuum. The teacher can subtly guide these conversations if needed, but student buy-in will be higher when students feel ownership over the creation process.

After the rubric has been sketched out, consider how the final product will be created. Some teachers create a large version and post it on a bulletin board in the classroom, while also giving students individual copies. Others simply distribute digital copies via the Learning Management System. Either way, a digital rubric maker will come in handy. There are several highly-touted and free rubric creators available. The most popular seem to be Rubric Maker (https://rubric-maker.com/) and Quick Rubric (https://www.quickrubric.com/).

Choice Boards

Rubrics are a perfect way to guide all types of alternative assessments. The best part of a great rubric is that it's product-agnostic—meaning the focus is on the learning, not the finished product. That works perfectly when it comes to giving students choice on how they will be assessed. Educators know that it's important to teach with various learning modalities and our learners' strengths in mind. Likewise, students need to be encouraged to demonstrate their learning in the modality that best serves them. Many times, teachers are a bit fearful of offering choices, thinking it will result in more work for them. If the rubric is well made, however, the number of choices won't matter. Instead, the results will be students who do not dread assessments, who do not get test anxiety, and who do not try to copy answers from their peers. On top of that, teachers will get examples of authentic learning experiences and a truer measure of growth. Multiple templates for choice boards are a simple Google search away. However, they are super easy to create from scratch, as well.

1.	Open a Microsoft Word or Google Doc
2.	Decide if you prefer portrait or landscape
3.	Decide on how many choices you are going to offer
4.	Insert a Table with that number of grids
5.	Start populating each box

It's that simple. You can get more creative by adding images into the boxes or filling the cells with various colors, but it's not necessary.

Table 6.1 How to Make a Student Choiceboard Using Microsoft Word or Google Docs

Figure 6.1 A QR Code to an example of a Choiceboard assignment with
Success Criteria

https://bit.ly/61FigureIWB

Digital Portfolios

Another example of an alternative assessment happens throughout the unit of teaching. Digital portfolios are an excellent way for students to demonstrate their learning over a period of time. Again, this begins with carefully planned success criteria and rubrics that provide clear direction to the students on what to include in their portfolios. Some teachers are hesitant to integrate performance tasks and Project Based learning experiences into the classroom because they fear a lack of assessment methods. Digital portfolios work extremely well in these scenarios. The students are able to select artifacts to include in their portfolios at specific benchmarks in the project, providing effective formative assessment data for the teacher throughout the entire experience. Not only are students selecting work that demonstrates their mastery of learning objectives, but they should also use their portfolios as a place to reflect on the learning process. Teachers may need to make this reflection more explicit by providing specific prompts at regular intervals for reflection. If students are already used to reflecting, it can be a more organic process.

There are very simple ways to create a digital portfolio like Google Slides and PowerPoint. There are two other EdTech tools that are favorites of many teachers and also offer a simple alternative: Canva and Adobe Express. Both of these platforms offer numerous visually appealing templates for students to start from and continue to build out their portfolios. Just like with choice boards, teachers can offer choices for how/where students create their digital portfolios. Not only are these a great alternative assessment choice, but they make fantastic artifacts for student-led conferences with parents, as well. Students will put more effort into their portfolios when they know the audience goes beyond their teachers.

When approaching assessment, many educators resort to whatever assessments they have used in the past because it makes sense and allows them to maintain a semblance of control; the feedback provided may not always be the most relevant to dictate future lessons, but it gives educators the basic feedback they need to wrap up a lesson and move to the next one. This last school year has greatly illuminated the need for transformation in regard to assessment, and much of the conversation across the educational landscape is turning to the idea of offering assessments that are meaningful to both the educator and the learner. It has become clear that educators often leave out a few integral ideas when planning assessments; moving forward, educators everywhere can maximize learning by considering variety and personalization while planning their assessments.

Alternatives to Traditional Writing Assignments and Assessments

In many humanities classes, writing is a commonplace assessment that happens at various times throughout the course of a unit; these writing assessments vary based on the objective, but can include quick write check-ins, short constructed responses, or even full-length essays. Unfortunately, sometimes this approach is not what is best for all learners and can get monotonous. In an effort to allow students to exemplify their learning or understanding of a concept in a way that is meaningful for them, it is important to give students an alternative to writing, and there are a variety of options that can meet the needs of different learners.

Photo Essay

For your visual learners, an effective approach could be asking the students to complete a photo essay. Photo essays allow students to share their understanding and insight and tell a story in a visual manner. Essentially, the goal would be for students to methodically choose and organize a series of photos that invite the audience along. The goal of a photo essay is to arrange the photos in a way that follows the narrative arc, exemplifies the tone and emotions of the experience, as well as sets the scene in a manner that requires no words. Photo essays are just a different approach to storytelling and provide an opportunity for learners to demonstrate their understanding of the concepts being discussed in a visual manner.

Photo essays are typically used when focusing on storytelling or narrative writing, but can also be applied to informational and argumentative writing as well. The slight tweak that might make all the difference could be to ask students to add short captions to the photos they choose in an effort to make the visual message clearer. Additionally, another approach could be to ask students to create their photo essay and then complete a screen share video recording or use Adobe Express Video to add voice-over and explanation. If you are worried you won't be able to fully assess student understanding simply based on the pictures selected, an accompanying video recording explanation can alleviate some of the confusion and provide a clear perspective.

Blogging

Instead of just completing a final written assessment at the end of a unit, another approach is allowing students to create an ongoing blog over the course of a unit. Typically, quick writes are used to introduce the lesson for the day or pre-emptively used to encourage thinking surrounding a topic before you launch into the lesson, but blogging (a series of quick writes) can consistently be used at the beginning, middle, or end of a unit or lesson. Educators can encourage ownership and engagement while gauging understanding surrounding a concept by letting students create, design, and maintain their blogs. Both teacher and peer feedback can be collected on these blogs, which encourages growth and reflection. Blogs can be used in all subjects and, when completed digitally, can give educators quick insight into knowing where student understanding may be. For example, say a world language educator is using a series of blog posts throughout their unit on "items found in the home." Often, the educator will require the students to use a list of commonly-used vocabulary terms in an accurate way to exemplify their understanding of the terminology; traditionally, this is a longer writing assignment collected at the end of a unit. If an educator assigns a series of blog posts that requires certain vocabulary to be used but also allows students to personalize the written expression, the educator is not only personalizing the assessment based on student background but is also providing an opportunity to get to know the student and can use the ctrl/cmd+F function to seek out the specific vocabulary being used in the assignment. Blogging is usually more informal than your typical essay, which for some might be problematic, but it doesn't need to take the place of traditional composition, but can absolutely supplement it throughout. By allowing students to complete a series of written assignments throughout the course of a unit/lesson, the educator can quickly provide on-the-spot feedback and redirection (if needed) rather than wait until the end of the unit to find out the students don't understand the concepts and it is too late to reteach before moving on to the next unit. Some educators might feel that grading a series of blog posts will require way too much time and there won't be an efficient way to get through the pages of writing; however, instead of grading every single post, educators can ask the students to review their blog posts and identify the top 2 or 3 they are most proud of and tag those specifically posts to be graded. One could even take it a step further and have students choose two posts, one they would like to receive a score, and one they would like to receive written or verbal (using Mote) feedback on; this approach encourages students to revisit their work and have some ownership in the scoring process.

Note: Microsoft One Note Notebook can be organized by sections and pages within that section so you can use it as an ongoing blog throughout the course of the year for each unit of study.

1. File > New Notebook
2. Select Color of Notebook, Title it, press Create
3. Hover over "New Section 1" and right-click to select rename and label it for your unit (eg. Unit 1: Contact to Seven Years War, Unit 2: A New Nation, Unit 3: Building a Democracy, etc.)
4. Hover over "Untitled Page" and right-click to select rename and label it for your lesson (eg. Blog Post #1, the blog post question/ topic, etc)
5. Move to the far right panel and start crafting the blog post
   a. Title at the top and body of text below

A couple of notes:
- Additionally, you can add images, files, links, drawings, equations, stickers, and audio to the blog posts directly in One Note by clicking the menu options at the top (Insert, Draw, View, Audio)
- One Note has the built-in Immersive Reader for accessibility purposes
- One Note allows for sharing and collaborating so teams or pairs could write collaborative blog posts or the notebook link can easily be uploaded to the LMS for educators to score
- One Note has an online option that makes it portable for students and does not need to be downloaded as a desktop application

Table 6.2 Setting up a Blog using Microsoft One Note

Conducting an Interview

In an effort to promote critical thinking skills, assess content knowledge understanding, as well as encourage the cultivation of soft skills like effective communication, active listening, and empathy, there is no better assessment than assigning your students to conduct interviews. In this process, students are able to craft questions that are meaningful and demonstrate their understanding of concepts; if students are uncertain about the content, their questions will demonstrate that by being simplistic or vague. However, by establishing a few parameters for question construction, educators can gauge the students' levels of understanding in a quick and more hands-off way. Students will likely not view the process as an assessment because they are getting a choice in how to proceed with the interview. Interviews can be conducted with community members, family, friends, or peers. Interview-style activities are a great way to get students interested in the lesson while also providing clear observational data for the educator on individual students and whole class understanding.

One interview-style activity that is engaging and exciting for students is modeled after the concept called Speed Dating. In this activity, the classroom is set up where two desks are across from each other and set up in a circle to mimic the idea of rotation (see Figure 6.2 below). Each round consists of 2-3 minutes of dialogue, and then a call for rotation is made where both parties rotate one seat to their right. If a classroom is 1:1, students can record their partner's answers on a digital document and synthesize the experience after class as a reflection activity. In a virtual setting, breakout rooms can be used to move the students from conversation to conversation, or a digital meeting space such as KumoSpace (https://www.kumospace.com/) or Spatial Chat (https://spatial.chat/) (Note: neither are made specifically for education and so must be monitored closely.) Prior to the activity, each individual student can be assigned a persona (e.g., a Famous Historian, Scientist, Mathematician, or Character from a text) to assume and generate a set number of questions about a concept or time period written from the perspective of their assigned persona. They can then take turns working through the Speed Dating activity, where they will get the chance to learn about a variety of individuals from a given time period. Additionally, the educator could choose a group of personas from a set time period or culture and require that the questions are focused on a specific topic. While the educator circulates the room, they can listen to the conversations and assess the mastery of the students.

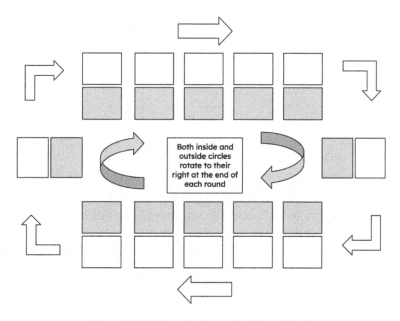

Figure 6.2 Collaborative Interview Speed-Dating

THE RESEARCH - FEEDBACK

Feedback is the result of an assessment. As we have learned, assessment takes place all of the time in classrooms, which now allows teachers to provide feedback at almost any time during synchronous or asynchronous instruction. What is feedback? Feedback provides our students with clarity on what good performance looks like in relation to the lesson or task goals (Nicol & McFarlane-Dick, 2006). Feedback also allows teachers and students to dialogue around what learning looks like during the lesson and task, which helps a teacher close gaps between current and desired performance in addition to helping teachers shape their instruction. Furthermore, feedback allows our students an opportunity to further develop as a learner. Much of the feedback research focuses on five key principles that allow for feedback to be useful for our learners. Our goal is to outline these five key principles of what feedback looks like before discussing different types of feedback as well as what the research says about providing feedback with EdTech tools.

Five Key Principles of Feedback Research

There are five key principles we can provide for our students. These overarching principles create a framework where feedback can be effective and manageable for students.

Focus on the Task

First, we want to focus the feedback directly on the task, not the learner. During this time, a teacher can focus on providing suggestions for the learner to improve (Butler, 1987; Narciss & Huth, 2004). For example, if it is a writing task, we focus specifically on the writing task and its requirements. Additionally, consider the evaluation of a math problem—task-based feedback would include outlining small suggestions on how to improve procedurally relating to how to solve the problem or find the errors made. Ultimately, this helps students see what needs to be done next to improve their ability to solve the problem at hand as well as similar types of problems.

Elaborate Feedback

Second, we want to give students elaborate feedback to enhance learning (Bangert-Drowns, Kulik & Morgan, 1991; Narciss & Huth, 2004; Shute, 2008). What does this mean and look like? To be specific, feedback should describe the *what*, *how*, and *why* of a given problem or task. Feedback should not be the verification of results, which is acknowledging they did a good job or made a mistake. For example, our feedback can look like telling our students what they may be missing on a task, how to get to the next step of solving a problem, and why the students may have made an error or completed the task with satisfactory performance in relation to the lesson's learning objectives.

Feedback in Manageable Amounts

Third, feedback must be given to students in manageable amounts. Feedback should be elaborated in small enough segments that it does not overwhelm learners or be disregarded by our students (Bransford, Bransford, Brown, & Cocking, 2000). Ultimately, if we provide too much feedback to our students, it may result in cognitive overload, which results in students not being able to process the information well (Mayer & Moreno, 2002). To alleviate this, teachers can provide feedback in a step-by-step process over time to give their students manageable units of information to correct their errors and heighten their performance in a task. For example, when giving students feedback relating to their writing, our feedback could relate to only one element of the writing sample for that specific draft. Or, when solving a math problem, our feedback relates to one step of the problem versus multiple steps of the problem.

Clear and Specific Feedback

Fourth, relating back to the third principle of feedback, our feedback must also be clear and specific and concurrently structured into units of manageable information. If our feedback is not specific or clear, our students may get flustered as well as impede their learning (Moreno, 2004; Wiliam, 2012). Therefore, we want our feedback to be clear and specific to goals and performance related to the task and lesson objective (Moreno, 2004; Wiliam, 2012). To illustrate this point, a student can solve a linear equation math problem. Say the student was not able to isolate the variable correctly, which caused them to get the remaining steps of the problem incorrect. If we focus on the part of the problem where they made the first initial error, we can tell them that ensuring the variable is isolated allows us to then find the ultimate solution to the problem at hand.

Feedback Must Meet the Learner's Needs

The fifth and final principle of feedback relates to providing feedback that meets the learner's needs (Kulhavy, White, Topp, Chan, & Adams, 1985). What this means is that we want our feedback to be simple and based on a single cue, verification, or hint. However, we need to have an idea of who the student is to whom we are giving feedback at that time. Ultimately, depending on the learner, they may require more complex feedback based on multiple cues (Kulhavy et al., 1985). But, for the most part, Kulhavy et al. (1985) suggest that our feedback should be more geared toward being simple than complex. Complex feedback does not promote learning in comparison to simple feedback.

Feedback is essential to developing our students and their abilities. To successfully provide feedback to students based on the five principles outlined above, we must focus directly on the task at hand; it must be elaborate and not simply of verification of an action taken by a student; feedback must be chunked into manageable pieces; it must be clear and specific; and we must give feedback that is specific to the learner and their needs. When these principles are integrated into our instruction, we can support students in learning the content and skills we want them to learn.

Types of Feedback: Formative and Summative Feedback

There are two major types of feedback we will be discussing in this chapter, which are summative and formative feedback. First, our goal will be to define summative and formative feedback. However, our primary focus will be on formative feedback as it is much more effective and engaging for students to receive than summative feedback (Rawle, Thuna, Zhao, & Kaler, 2018).

Summative feedback is feedback given to students after a unit of study, semester, or school year. Typically, summative feedback looks like a progress report, report card, or summative assessment or project. Summative feedback generally is an all-encompassing indicator that relates to the level of achievement made in relation to the learning objectives and standards presented. While it is important to summarize student progress, the feedback that is most effective is formative assessment (Davies, 2011; Graham, 2015; Huxham, 2007; Liu & Lee, 2013). Therefore, as we frame our conversation, formative feedback will be the focus.

Formative Feedback

Formative feedback is considered an informal or low-stakes opportunity to provide students with feedback, which can be used for students to understand where they are at in their learning and see how and where they can improve. Furthermore, formative feedback is our opportunity to provide students with personalized feedback that can be processed by a student to then be turned into an action to improve a skill or work product. This can be verbal, textual, video, or visual feedback, which can be done in the moment or during the course of synchronous and asynchronous instruction throughout the lesson or week, depending on the task being asked of students.

To be most effective with formative assessment, we must develop routines for students to do something with the feedback we give them (Davies, 2011). If our feedback is left without a task to reinforce it, our feedback may be neglected and not taken into consideration by students. Thus, routines such as having students comment back and discuss how they used the feedback in their writing, showing us they were able to solve the next step or entire math problem, or sharing with us learning reflections after the lesson has been completed related to what they learned and how they processed and utilized our feedback are all routines we can develop to ensure feedback is being used by our students.

Beyond routines, there are a few things we can do to make our formative feedback effective. First, if we give our students personalized feedback, it will motivate students to do better (Graham, 2015). For example, always use a student's name and personalize the feedback to the task the student is completing. Second, try to give students feedback in a timely manner, as it will have a more significant impact on learning the sooner it has been given (Huxham, 2007). The third and most important aspect of formative feedback is to align it to clear learning objectives and criteria related to the task or assignment, followed by instructions on how to improve (Liu & Lee, 2013). The use of teacher and student rubrics that are aligned to the objectives of the lesson and standard allows for students to know what is expected. Additionally, verbal, written, or video instructions on how to improve that are derived from the feedback will help students know what to do next with the feedback they have received.

Formative feedback is essential in modern classroom settings. As we will soon discuss, there are many ways teachers can provide effective feedback to the vast majority of their students efficiently and timely. EdTech has allowed for the formative assessment and feedback to occur simultaneously, which gives teachers an assortment of tools to monitor student progress and adjust their instruction.

Effective Feedback Using EdTech as a Delivery Method

To finalize research about feedback, we wanted to focus on how we can harness EdTech to allow teachers to be efficient in giving feedback as well as providing effective feedback. EdTech allows teachers to expand their feedback by giving them a multitude of different mediums to create feedback for their students. These mediums of feedback can include text, audio, video, and visual feedback. With the help of dashboards on many of our EdTech tools, we can create and deliver feedback to our students. Dashboards, in this case, can be on an LMS or on a single tool itself, which then can be delivered to students working on that specific tool. Also, feedback developed on specific tools can be outsourced to different platforms (i.e., generally video and audio feedback) for students to review. Our goal is to give a summary of the research on how we can use EdTech tools and their dashboards effectively to create and deliver feedback to students. Then, we will focus on the best mediums of feedback that can be created with EdTech tools that can improve student learning.

Dashboards are interfaces that allow teachers to analyze student activity, review data, manage deploying content, and provide feedback. With the advent of dashboards, we now have the ability to increase the amount of feedback given to students as well as elicit more effective types of feedback (Knoop-van Campsen & Molenaar, 2020). When using a dashboard, the principles of feedback as discussed earlier apply and have been shown to create positive benefits to student learning because the feedback was personalized, within a sequence related to the task, and timely (Knoop Campen & Molenaar, 2020).

Mediums of feedback have exponentially increased as a result of EdTech. We have textual, audio, visual, and video feedback that can be created on numerous tools. However, in terms of the most engaging and personalized mechanism to create effective feedback that is efficient to distribute, it's audio feedback. Audio feedback is the best medium available for teachers to overcome student disengagement as well as direct students with informative feedback to improve (Rawle, Thuna, Zhao, & Kaler, 2018).

INSTRUCTIONAL STRATEGY INTEGRATION WITH EDTECH TOOLS TO AMPLIFY LEARNING: FEEDBACK

Immediately after a form of assessment has occurred, feedback should be a major focus. Additionally, as you plan the types of assessments you want to integrate into your instruction, the feedback generated as a result of the assessment should be at the forefront of your thoughts. Ultimately, our assessments are only as good as the feedback we provide to our students as a result of the assessment. As we discuss types of feedback we can integrate with EdTech tools into our instruction, we will be discussing examples of informal feedback, rubrics for feedback, and student feedback to teachers. Each feedback topic discussed will outline several EdTech tools that can be utilized to generate feedback for our students that can be deployed during live synchronous instruction or during asynchronous instruction. The themes of instructional strategy and EdTech integrations will focus on the following:

1. Ways and Mediums to Deliver Feedback to Students
2. Student and Teacher Rubrics
3. Student to Teacher Feedback

Overall, the goal of each integration is to show you how to provide feedback in a multitude of ways that is effective and aligns with the research. As you review the following EdTech integrations with the strategies, evaluate which integrations will work best for providing your students with feedback that they can do something with to extend their learning.

Informal Feedback

There are many types of feedback including: written, video, and verbal. Sometimes the informal, in-the-moment feedback can be the most constructive for students. The best way to deliver informal feedback is during organic conversations and during one-on-one conferences between teacher and student or among peers. These conversations help build rapport and typically have a higher buy-in from students because they are part of a discussion and not just a receiver of information. When people can't have these conversations face-to-face, there are EdTech tools that help provide a similar feel in order to still provide some informal feedback.

Screencasts are easy to create and don't require much planning on the teacher's part. Teachers can do a quick video record sharing their screen or utilizing their webcams to provide quick verbal feedback to share with the student. This also works well to provide feedback to a group of students who are working collaboratively on a project. Screencastify is a Chrome extension that is easy to install and even easier to use.

Mote is another great Chrome extension that can be used to provide quick informal feedback. With Mote, teachers and students can easily record audio clips within a Google Doc, an assignment, or an email. Many of today's learners provide verbal feedback to written, making Mote more attractive than comments written onto an assignment.

Rubrics for Feedback

In an effort to put the onus on the student and encourage ownership over their own learning, an educator might consider putting a non-traditional spin on the typical rubric. Rubrics are generally thought of as something used in an English class, but the reality is that any subject can benefit from the use of rubrics. Rubrics afford clear understanding and communication from the teacher to the learner. Unlike written or qualitative feedback, rubrics are grounded in quantitative data established by clear metrics that build on each other. If an educator simply resorts to assigning a score, the student never really gains an understanding as to what they are doing well or what they can improve upon; even if an educator adds written comments on the assignment to guide the student, it is common that the students gloss over the written feedback in search of the numerical score that will be added to the grade book. Rubrics combine the written feedback that an educator wants the student to reflect on and that score that students seek out. The first step in choosing a rubric is considering the best fit for the assignment; educators can choose from a variety of rubrics ranging from a standards-based rubric to analytic rubrics to holistic rubrics. These rubrics can be applied to written, oral, visual, et cetera assignments and have clear-cut criteria that differ across scoring items. Educators can either create their own rubrics, or if they are interested in using a template, they can use an online rubric generator, such as RubiStar (http://rubistar. 4teachers.org), which provides a template based on the subject being assessed. Additionally, most LMS systems (e.g., Google Classroom, Schoology, Canvas, et cetera) have built-in rubric generators that can be used as great feedback tools for digital assignments.

Speaking and listening is one area where educators don't think twice about using rubrics, but they can be beneficial to provide a clear understanding as to where students can improve. Many students don't consider speaking and listening skills as important as content knowledge or traditional academic skills, but speaking and listening are essential to success in many industries. The first step to creating a speaking and listening rubric includes identifying the important speaking and listening skills an educator wants to observe during the activity. Take, for example, a Philosophical Chairs debate. In this debate, individuals follow a back-and-forth structure that includes perspective generation, active listening, paraphrasing, questioning, synthesizing, building on others' ideas, et cetera.

Rules of Philosophical Chairs

1. Make sure you understand the question before you decide whether you agree or disagree.
2. Face each other across the center of the room depending on your response.
3. THINK before you SPEAK and organize your thoughts and ideas.
4. Briefly summarize the previous speaker's points before stating your own comments.
5. Address the ideas, not the person.
6. After speaking, WAIT until at least ONE students from your side speaks before speaking again. *Don't monopolize though!
7. One speaker at a time, others are listeners. You can't be the speaker unless you have the "talking ball."
8. Feel free to switch sides if you are compelled.

Figure 6.3 Rules of Philosophical Chairs

So, an educator would consider all those qualities, create a clear rubric with clear criteria, review it with the students before the activity, and then score the students as they share. You can see an example of a speaking and listening rubric below in Figure 6.4.

Criteria	1	2	3	4	5
Summary of Previous Person's Ideas	**Not Used=** Did not do any summary	**Little Used=** Had reference, but not information	**Acceptable Use=** Made reference and included facts	**Excellent Use=** Restated arguments and included facts	**Outstanding Use=** Restated arguments and ALL facts
Thoughtful Reflection	**Not Used=** Did not have understanding of the topic	**Little Used=** Had superficial understanding of the topic	**Acceptable Use=** Understand topic well enough to explain own argument	**Excellent Use=** Explained most of complexity of the topic	**Outstanding Use=** Complexity of the topic explained and used arguments
Use Specific Examples	**Not Used=** No examples used	**Little Used=** One example used, but no elaboration	**Acceptable Use=** Examples used with some explanation	**Excellent Use=** Examples used and explanation had some depth	**Outstanding Use=** Examples used, each explained in depth, and it was extended to fit the argument
Usage and Grammar	**Not Used=** Errors in agreement and non-standard English	**Little Used=** Informal English and words like "you know" and "thing"	**Acceptable Use=** Standard English usage and complete ideas	**Excellent Use=** Standard English usage with no mistakes and with use of some allusions	**Outstanding Use=** Standard English usage with no mistakes and the use of allusions and precise references to develop arguments

Figure 6.4 Speaking and Listening Rubric

Another important approach to feedback that generates high levels of engagement and depth in critical thinking is activities that ask students to assess their learning on a rubric and then compare it with a rubric completed by their teacher. By asking the students to step into the assessor's shoes, they will gain clarity about the process of assessment and feedback; they will be able to give an honest glimpse into their own learning and provide the educator with a greater understanding as to whether or not the learner had a true understanding of the task at hand based on their self-assessment. If teacher and student find they are widely disparate in their assessment, this has the capacity to open a dialogue into strengths and weaknesses as well as forces the student to think about their level of effort and understanding.

Student Feedback to the Teacher

We've spent a large amount of time discussing the value of students *receiving* feedback, but it's also important to give them a voice in *giving* feedback to their teachers. Effective teachers do a good job of reflecting on lessons and adjusting/changing for the following year. However, if students are not given a voice in that reflection, the most important perspective is often lost. Teachers can collect student feedback on specific lessons by adding an additional question to the end of a reflection from (i.e., Google Forms or Microsoft Forms), and they can gather bigger picture feedback through other methods throughout or at the end of a semester.

Teachers can have students complete end-of-semester surveys, write anonymous notes, or take part in a focus group to share feedback. In a classroom where strong relationships have been cultivated, students will feel more comfortable giving honest feedback to the teacher. The key is for teachers to accept that feedback and reflect on how they can use it to strengthen their craft.

CONCLUSION—THE AGE OF FORMATIVE ASSESSMENT AND FEEDBACK

Throughout this chapter, we discussed how assessment and feedback are both critical elements of our instruction. In our lesson planning, our assessments should align with how we are going to be delivering student feedback. Luckily, many EdTech tool integrations have allowed for this to be done in tandem by assessing students and then providing feedback in the form of whole class feedback and personalized individual feedback. Now, this can be done in a matter of seconds or minutes with the tools we have at our disposal.

However, even with the advent of new tools that have revolutionized the way we can assess and provide feedback, we must look at the research closely to ensure we are strategic in how we are assessing students and providing feedback. Ultimately, we want to be efficient and effective with our assessment, which makes formative assessment a powerful mechanism to assess students quickly. It also provides effective options for giving the whole class personalized feedback. It must be noted that formative assessment can take different forms and can be scaffolded over time to create student artifacts such as digital portfolios. Therefore, our mindsets related to traditional forms of formative and summative assessment need to change. Our goal throughout this chapter was to exemplify how the options for assessment have changed and expanded as a result of technology.

Feedback has manifested into text, images, audio, and video that can be delivered at a single time, but also archived so they can be long-standing forms of feedback students can always look back upon as they progress through the curriculum. Additionally, feedback can be delivered to students within multiple classroom settings at once. Students can be within an online and in-person setting and receive the same form of feedback simultaneously. Also, students can provide their own teacher's feedback throughout the course of the year if the option is provided. Altogether, the opportunities for providing feedback are immense. When delivered with intent and strategically, our feedback can increase the learning of our students within modern classroom settings.

CONTINUING THE CONVERSATION—NEXT STEPS

Directions: After reading Chapter Six, take a moment and write down one to three strategies discussed regarding assessment and feedback. Then, discuss how they may look in your classroom when you try them. Last, outline what steps you need to take to make them a reality in your classroom. Share your thoughts with your PLN with the hashtag #**InstructWithoutBoundaries.**

Formative Assessment Strategies
Feedback Strategies
Next Steps Toward Implementation

CONCLUSION— INSTRUCTION WITHOUT BOUNDARIES

ENHANCE YOUR TEACHING STRATEGIES WITH TECHNOLOGY TOOLS IN ANY SETTING

Every educator, despite location, despite years in service, despite teaching philosophy, aims to provide their students with the highest quality learning experience they can; for many, this goal moves beyond just a job and has become a duty they consider worthwhile and of utmost importance. Each educator who enters the profession enters with a vigor that fuels their desire to transform the face of education, and each educator who eventually retires desires to do so knowing they had an impact that is profound and one that has left a legacy of learning that exceeds their young self's expectations.

Every educator has the opportunity to set their students up for success and place them on a positive trajectory of lifelong learning that will enhance their experience beyond their educational career, but it begins with a shift. As education evolves, we must evolve as well. The reality is this: educators everywhere are doing great things for their students, and while the EdTech tools might change over time, the instructional strategies have proven beneficial time and time again. So draw upon what works, but realize that sometimes what works could even use some elevation at times. Every student deserves to be that second hypothetical student outlined in the introduction of this book. Every student should be given a chance to be an active participant in their own learning. They deserve to be engaged. They deserve to have the chance to collaborate with peers. They deserve the opportunity to be critical thinkers and broaden their view of the world. Additionally, they deserve to be provided a place where their creative selves can flourish. It is our responsibility to shift for the sake of our students, and that isn't something we should take lightly.

This book has outlined a series of instructional approaches that are ripe with strategies and activities that traverse instructional boundaries; the onus for growth and evolution rests in your hands— do not let it pass you by. Take what you know as an amazing educator, use tools like those in this book to amplify the instruction, and watch as your classroom of scholars transforms for the better.

Why Should We Care—A Pathway Forward for Instruction Without Boundaries

Learning instructional strategies to integrate with EdTech tools is essential for creating classrooms without boundaries where instruction transcends and moves between digital and physical spaces. In our current world of education, our classrooms do not need four walls. Rather, the entire world is interconnected by the internet and technology, which can be the infrastructure for modern classrooms. However, as technology is constantly changing and the tools we use eventually go out of date, it is important for us to know instructional strategies that help us learn. As we have learned, the EdTech tools may increase the learning taking place, but the instructional strategies are foundational to allow the tool to amplify the learning taking place. As a result, as the tools change, we can use many of the same research-based strategies with the new EdTech tools that are developed.

Classrooms without boundaries are the future and are becoming ever more the reality in the world we live in. While there will always be an aspect of in-person learning taking place within groups of students at a physical school, we are moving further into a world where learning can take place at any time and anywhere. As a result, teachers and school leaders must be prepared to deliver instruction in this world, which means instruction can take place purely online, within a blended learning setting, or fully in-person. Also, throughout a school year or perhaps at the drop of a hat, teachers may have to move their instruction into one or more of these settings. With a solid foundation of strategies that can be integrated with a wide range of EdTech tools, this is very doable and something we can all do in creative and innovative ways to amplify our students' learning.

When thinking about classrooms without boundaries, we also must think that this is not just an isolated event taking place in North America. The advancements in technology are global, and sooner or later, each part of the globe will have the ability within their education systems to create and maintain classrooms without boundaries. While this will manifest itself at different times in the 2020s in places around the world, the benefits will be seen by millions of teachers and students as classrooms without boundaries are far more equitable and inclusive than classrooms with boundaries. Students who have access to devices and the internet have the opportunity to see the world, create things that may impact the world, and connect with their classmates, other students around the world, and experts in various fields of interest. At no time in history has this been possible within our classrooms. Ultimately, the possibilities are endless for our classrooms and students when the learning opportunities are all around us, interconnected across the globe!

Practical Steps: Taking the Learning Beyond Reading

We all want to foster self-directed learning in our students. Fortunately, we also have the power to design and develop our own self-directed learning experience. Think less is more, and choose one or two chapters from the book to incorporate first into your practice. All of the strategies discussed are important and play a part in every classroom, but be strategic in your implementation. Take time to try something, make adjustments, try it again, and continue the process until you and your students are comfortable. Little by little, you'll find yourself applying the concepts over time.

Similarly, setting goals and creating an action plan is key to your own professional growth. Maybe you want to increase student collaboration in your classroom. Craft that idea into a measurable goal, and then write action steps to help you fulfill your goal. Action plans should be active and growing throughout the process. After you've completed an action plan, set aside time for intentional reflection. Some educators prefer to reflect on their own through writing, drawing, or even video recording their thoughts. Other people reflect better with an accountability partner or even an entire PLC group. It doesn't matter how you reflect, but it does matter that you **do** reflect. Those reflections are the deepest learning and will continue to guide you toward accomplishing your goal. And the beautiful part about goals is that they *can* be changed. This is *your* plan, developed by you and for you, so feel free to adjust it as many times as you need to.

Avenues to Continue Learning

There are so many ways to continue learning while you are working toward your goals, and finding a thought partner that has a foundation in the book can lead to powerful growth and application.

Conversations in the hallway	<ul><li>Share what you've learned</li><li>How you are applying it</li><li>How your students are responding</li></ul>
Give the book away	<ul><li>Pass the book on to another educator</li><li>Engage them in conversations to compare thinking and learning</li></ul>
Website	<ul><li>Sign up for our newsletter</li><li>Check out our speaking schedule</li><li>Watch for opportunities for online courses</li></ul>
Share with your PLN	<ul><li>Join a book study</li><li>Engage in a Twitter Chat</li><li>Post on Instagram</li><li>Share in a Facebook Group</li></ul>

A CALL TO ACTION

The strategies discussed in this book are timeless and will be further developed by additions to the body of research. Therefore, while the EdTech tools may change over time, always focus on the instructional strategies. This is one of the major reasons we focused on the instructional strategies, the research behind them, and how to incorporate them into our instruction before our secondary focus was on integrating them with EdTech tools. The goal was to demonstrate instructional strategies can be utilized within any classroom setting and can be effective with a wide range of tools. As a result, this creates classroom environments that can take place anywhere and at any time. This is what classrooms without boundaries are about!

So as you think about your practice, consider areas that could use improvement, and do not be afraid to change and tweak for the betterment of the student experience. Often, change automatically equals bad in the eyes of individuals, but change does not always have to be a bad thing. Change is an opportunity for individuals to evolve and transform. We would be doing a disservice if we didn't highlight the fact that while change can be good, it is often challenging. So, as you evaluate what works in your classroom practice and note some areas for growth, always keep in mind, there will be growing pains throughout the process. Embrace those moments because, as history has shown, moments of struggle often lead to eventual strength. Keep pressing forward, knowing that the outcome is worth the process, and watch your students thrive!

REFERENCES

Abed, A. Z., Sameer, S. A., Kasim, M. A., & Othman, A. T. (2019). Predicting effect implementing the jigsaw strategy on the academic achievement of students in mathematics classes. *International Electronic Journal of Mathematics Education, 15*(1), em0558.

Akhand, M. M. (2015). Project based learning (PBL) and webquest: New dimensions in achieving learner autonomy in a class at tertiary level. *Journal of Pan-Pacific Association of Applied Linguistics, 19*(2),55-74.Retrieved from http://www.eric.ed.gov/contentdelivery/servlet/ERIC-Servlet?accno=EJ1092455

Alfares, N. (2017). Benefits and difficulties of learning in group work in EFL classes in Saudi Arabia. *English Language Teaching, 10*(7), 247-256.

Alioon, Y. & Delialioğlu, Ö. (2019). The effect of authentic e-learning activities on student engagement and motivation. *British Journal of Educational Technology, 50*(2): 655–668. DOI: https://doi.org/10.1111/ bjet.12559

Anthony, E. (2019). Blended learning: How traditional best teaching practices impact blended elementary classrooms. *Journal of Online Learning Research, 5*(1) 248.

Armellini, A., & Aiyegbayo, O. (2010). Learning design and assessment with e-tivities. *British Journal of Educational Technology, 41*(6), 922-935.

Aronson, E., Stephen, C., Sikes, J., Blaney, N., & Snapp, M. (1978). *The jigsaw classroom.* Beverly Hills, CA: Sage.

Baer, J. (2010). Is creativity domain specific? *In J.C. Kaufman & R.J. Sternberg (Eds), The Cambridge handbook of creativity* (pp. 321-341). Cambridge, NY: Cambridge UP.

Banchi, H., & Bell, R. (2008). The many levels of inquiry. *Science and Children, 46*(2), 26-29. Retrieved from https://www. proquest.com/scholarly-journals/many-levels-inquiry/ docview/236901022/se-2?accountid=193987

Bangert-Drowns, R. L., Kulik, C. L. C., Kulik, J. A., & Morgan, M. (1991). The instructional effect of feedback in test-like events. *Review of Educational Research, 61*(2), 213-238.

Barrett, H. (2003). Presentation at first International conference on the e-Portfolio, Poiters, France, October 9, 2003. [Retrieved January 21, 2005, from: http://electronicportfolios.org/portfolios/eifel.pdf]

Billings, L. & Fitzgerald, J. (2002). Dialogic discussion and the Paideia seminar. *American Educational Research Journal, 39*(4), 907-941.

Blatchford, P., Kutnick, P., Baines, E., & Galton, M. (2003). Toward a social pedagogy of classroom group work. *International Journal of Educational Research, 39*, 153–172.

Boden, M. A. (2004). *The creative mind: Myths and mechanisms* (2nd ed). London: Routledge.

Bodner, G. M. (1986). Constructivism: A theory of knowledge. *Journal of Chemical Education, 63*(10): 873–78. https://doi. org/10.1021/ed063p873

Bond, M., & Bedenlier, S. (2019). Facilitating student engagement through educational Technology: Toward a Conceptual Framework. *Journal of Interactive Media in Education, 1*(11), 1–14. DOI: https://doi.org/10.5334/jime.528

Bransford, J. D., Brown, A. L., & Cocking, R. R. (1999). The design of learning environments. *How People Learn: Brain, Mind, Experience, and School*, 117-142.

Brown, S. & Knight, P. (1998) *Assessing Learners in Higher Education*. Philadelphia: Routledge.

Bruen, J., Crosbie, V., Kelly, N., Loftus, M., Maillot, A., McGillicuddy, Á., & Pechenart, J. (2016). Teaching controversial topics in the humanities and social sciences in Ireland: Using structured academic controversy to develop multi-perspectivity in the learner. *JSSE-Journal of Social Science Education, 15*(3), 18-25.

Butler, R. (1987). Task-involving and ego-involving properties of evaluation: Effects of different feedback conditions on motivational perceptions, interest, and performance. *Journal of educational psychology, 79*(4), 474.

Cameron, C. E., Conner, C. M, Morrison, F. J. & Jewkes, A. M. (2008). Effects of classroom organization on letter-word reading in first grade. *Journal of School Psychology, 46*(2), 173-192.

Chan, C. K. (2001). Peer collaboration and discourse patterns in learning from incompatible information. *Instructional Science, 29*(6), 443-479.

Clark, D. (2010). *Bloom's taxonomy of learning domains: The three types of learning*. Retrieved from http://www.nwlink.com/~donclark/hrd/bloom.html

Clark, J.E. (2009). E-portfolios at 2.0: Surveying the field. *Association of American Colleges and Universities Peer Review, 11*(1), 1,4.

Chatterji, A. K. (2018). Innovation and American K–12 education. *Innovation Policy and the Economy, 18*(1), 27-51.

Cheng, K. (2006). Does cooperative learning enhance the residual effects of student interpersonal relationship skills? A case study at a Taiwan Technical College. *The Journal of American Academy of Business, 10*(1), 312-316.

Chidozie, C. C., Yusri, K., Muhammad Sukri, S., & Wilfredo, L.H. (2014). Implementing higher-order thinking skills in teaching and learning of design and technology education [Conference Presentation]. *International Seminar Proceedings on Technical and Vocational Education.* Bandung, Indonesia.

Chiriac, E. H., & Granström, K. (2012). Teachers' leadership and students' experience of group work. *Teachers and Teaching, 18*, 345–363.

Colbeck, C. L., Campbell, S. E., & Bjorklund, S. A. (2000).Grouping in the dark: What college students learn from group projects. *The Journal of Higher Education, 71*(1), 60–83. doi:10.2307/2649282

Darling-Hammond, L. (2012). *Powerful teacher education: Lessons from exemplary programs.* New York, NY: John Wiley & Sons.

Davies, A. (2011). Making classroom assessment work (3rd ed.). Courtenay, BC:Connect2learning.

Dickson, W. P. (2005). *Toward a deeper understanding of student performance in virtual high school courses: Using quantitative analyses and data visualization to inform decision making.* Lansing, MI: Michigan Virtual University. Retrieved from http://www.mivu.org/LinkClick.aspx?fileticket=15uq2DZ7Y+I=&tabbid=373.

DiCarlo, K., & Cooper, L. (2014). Classroom assessment techniques: A literature review. *Journal of Instructional Research, 3*, 15-20.

Delaney, T. A., & Hata, M. (2020). Universal design for learning in assessment: Supporting ELLs with learning disabilities. *Latin American Journal of Content & Language Integrated Learning, 13*(1) 79-91.

Dempsey, J. V. (1993). *Interactive instruction and feedback*. Englewood Cliffs, NJ: Educational Technology Publications.

D'Eon, M., & Proctor, P. (2001). An innovative modification to structured controversy. *Innovations in Education and Teaching International, 38*(3), 251-256.

Dewey, J (1997) [1938]. Experience and education: *The Kappa Delta Pi Lecture Series*. New York, NY: Touchstone.

Doymus, K. (2008). Teaching chemical equilibrium with the jigsaw technique. *Research in science Education, 38*(2), 249-260.

Ducasse, A. M., & Hill, K. (2019). Developing student feedback literacy using educational technology and the reflective feedback conversation. *Practitioner Research in Higher Education, 12*(1), 24-37.

Dufva, T. (2017). Maker movement creating knowledge through basic intention. *Techne Series: Research in Sloyd Education and Craft Science A, 24*(2) 130-141.

EdTech Review. (2013, April 23). What is GBL (Game-based Learning)? Retrieved May 13, 2022, from http://edtechreview.in/dictionary/298-what-is-game-based-learning

Farah, N. & Ayoubi, Z. (2020). Enhancing the critical thinking skills of grade 8 chemistry students using an inquiry and reflection teaching method. *Journal of Education in Science, Environment and Health (JESEH), 6*(3), 207-219. DOI:10.21891/jeseh.656872

Fisher, D., Frey, N., & Hattie, J. (2020). *The distance learning playbook, grades K-12: Teaching for engagement and impact in any setting*. Thousand Oaks, CA: Corwin Press.

Flavell, J. (1976). Metacognitive aspects of problem-solving. *In L. B. Resnick (Ed.), The nature of intelligence*. Hillsdale, NJ: Erlbaum

Forehand, M. (2010). *Bloom's taxonomy. Emerging perspectives on learning, teaching, and technology.* Retrieved from http:// projects.coe.uga.edu/epltt/index.php?title=Bloom% 27s_Taxonomy

Fredericks, J.A., Filsecker, J. Lawson, M. (2016). Student engagement, context and adjustment: Addressing definitional, measurement, and methodological issues. *Learning and Instruction, 43,* 1–4. DOI: https://doi.org/10.1016/j.learninstruc.2016.02.002

Freedman-Herreid, C. (2005.) Structured controversy, A case study strategy: DNA fingerprinting in the courts. *Case studies in Science: State University of New York at Buffalo.* Retrieved from sciencecases.lib.buffalo.edu/cs /pdfs/Structured%20Controversy-XXVI-2.pdf

Fredricks, J.A., Blumenfeld, P.C. & Paris, A.H. (2004). School engagement: Potential of the concept, state of the evidence. *Review of Educational Research, 74*(1): 59–109. DOI: https://doi. org/10.3102/00346543074001059

Frey, B., & Schmitt, V. (2010). Teachers' classroom assessment practices. *Middle Grades Research Journal, 5*(3), 107-117.

Fry, H., Ketteridge, S., & Marshall, S. (Eds.). (2008). *A handbook for teaching and learning in higher education: Enhancing academic practice.* UK: Routledge. https://doi.org/10.4324/ 9780203891414

Furtak, E. M., Seidel, T., Iverson, H., & Briggs, D. C. (2012). Experimental and quasi-experimental studies of inquiry-based science teaching: A meta-analysis. *Review of Educational Research, 82*(3), 300–329. doi:10.3102/0034654312457206

Gabbard, T., & Romanelli, F. (2021). Do student self-assessments of confidence and knowledge equate to competence? *American Journal of Pharmaceutical Education. 85*(4), 1-6.

Graham, B. (2015). Providing effective formative feedback. *BU Journal of Graduate Studies in Education, 7*(1), 35-39.

Hacker, D. (1998). Definitions and empirical foundations. In D. Hacker, J. Dunlosky, & A. Graesser (Eds.). *Metacognition in educational theory and practice.* Mahwah, NJ: Lawrence Erlbaum Associates, Publishers.

Hahn, C. (2009). Turning points as civic teaching moments. Paper presented at the conference, Turning points in civic education. *Bundeszentrale für politische Journal of Social Science Education, 15*(3). Retrieved from www.-civiced.org/pdfs/GermanAmerican Conf2009Sep/Hahn_C_Turning_Points.pdf

Hamane, A. C. (2014). Student engagement in an online course and its impact on student success. (Unpublished doctoral dissertation), Pepperdine University, Malibu, CA

Hamden, R. K. A. (2017). The effect of (Think-Pair-Share) strategy on the achievement of third grade student in sciences in the educational district of irbid. *Journal of Education and Practice, 8*(9), 88-95.

Han, S., & Yi, Y. (2009). English majors' writing course and the development of critical thinking skills. *Foreign Languages and Literature Studies, 1,* 24-28.

Harvard Graduate School of Education. (2015). *Circle of viewpoints.* Project Zero. http://www.pz.harvard.edu/resources/circle-of-viewpoints.

Hattie, J. (2009). *Visible learning: A synthesis of over 800 meta-analyses relating to achievement.* New York, NY: Routledge.

Hattie, J. (2012). *Visible Learning for teachers: Maximizing impact on learning.* New York, NY: Routledge.

Hawthorne, G., Quintin, E. M., Saggar, M., Bott, N., Keinitz, E., Liu, N., Reiss, A. L. (2014). Impact and sustainability of creative capacity building: The cognitive, behavioral, and neural correlates of increasing creative capacity. In L. Leifer, H. Plattner, & C. Meinel (Eds.), *Design thinking research* (pp. 65–77). Cham: Springer International Publishing.

Hill, N. E., & Taylor, L. C. (2004). Parental school involvement and children's academic achievement: Pragmatics and issues. *Current directions in psychological science, 13*(4), 161-164.

Hmelo-Silver, C.Y E. &. Barrows, H.S. (2008). Facilitating collaborative knowledge building. *Cognition and instruction, 26*(1), 48-94.

Holubec, E., Johnson, D. W., & Johnson, R. (1998). *Advanced cooperative learning* (3rd Edition). Edina, MN: Interaction Book Company.

Horn, M. B. & Stalker, H. (2015). *Blended: Using disruptive innovation to improve schools.* San Francisco, CA: JosseyBass.

Huxham, M. (2007). Fast and effective feedback: Are model answers the answer? *Assessment and Evaluation in Higher Education, 32*(6), 601-611. doi:10.1080/02602930601116946

Hughes, J., Morrison, L., Kajamaa, A., & Kumpulainen, K. (2018). Makerspaces promoting students' design thinking and collective knowledge creation: Examples from Canada and Finland. In *Interactivity, Game Creation, Design, Learning, and Innovation* (pp. 343-352). Edinburgh, UK: Springer, Cham.

Hyperdocs.co. (2021). *Hyperdocs.* Retrieved March 3, 2021, from https://Hyperdocs.co/

Institute of Design at Stanford. (2016). *An introduction to design thinking process guide.* Retrieved from http://dschool.stanford.edu/

Johnson, D. W., Johnson, R. T., & Smith. K. A. (2000). Constructive controversy. *Change, 32*(1), 28-37.

Jonassen, D., & Grabowski, B. (1993). *Handbook of individual differences, learning, and instruction.* Hillsdale, NJ: LEA.

Jerome, C., Lee, J. A., & Ting, S. (2017). What students really need: Instructional strategies that enhance higher order thinking skills (hots) among UNIMAS undergraduates. International

Journal of Business and Society, 18(4), 661-668. Retrieved from http://www.ijbs.unimas.my/images/repository/pdf/Vol18-s4-paper2.pdf

Kasof, J. (1997). Creativity and breadth of attention. *Creativity Research Journal, 10*(4), 303-315.

Kagan, S. (1989). The structural approach to cooperative learning. *Educational Leadership, 47*(4), 12-15.

King, F. J., Goodson, L., & Rohani, F. (2011). Higher order thinking skills: Definitions, strategies, assessment. Tallahassee, FL: Florida State University, Center for Advancement of Learning and Assessment.

Kirschner, P. A., Sweller, J., Kirschner, F., & Zambrano, J. (2018). From cognitive load theory to collaborative cognitive load theory. *International Journal of Computer-Supported Collaborative Learning, 13*(2), 213-233.

Kitot, A.K.A., Ahmad, A.R., & Seman, A.A. (2010). The effectiveness of inquiry teaching in enhancing students' critical thinking. *Procedia Social and Behavioral Sciences, 7,* 264-273.

Knoop-van Campen, C., & Molenaar, I. (2020). How teachers integrate dashboards into their feedback practices. *Frontline Learning Research, 8*(4), 37-51.

Kord Ali Gurk, N., & Mall-Amiri, B. (2016). The effect of cooperative learning techniques on intermediate Iranian EFL learners' reading comprehension and reading strategies. *Journal of Studies in Education, 6*(4), 33-59.

Kulhavy, R. W., White, M. T., Topp, B. W., Chan, A. L., & Adams, J. (1985). Feedback complexity and corrective efficiency. *Contemporary educational psychology, 10*(3), 285-291.

Kwok, A. P., & Lau, A. (2015). An exploratory study on using the think-pair-share cooperative learning strategy. *Journal of Mathematical Sciences. 2*, 22-28.

Lai, E., DiCerbo, K., & Foltz, P. (2017). *Skills for today: What we know about teaching and assessing collaboration.* New York, NY: Pearson.

Larson, L. C., & Miller, T. N. (2011). 21st-century skills: Prepare students for the future. *Kappa Delta Pi Record, 47*(3), 121-123.

Lawler, J. (2013). Engaging community service students through digital portfolios. *Information STEAMs Education Journal, 11*(1), 41.

Lawton, D., Vye, N., Bransford, J., Sanders, E., Richey, M., French, D., & Stephens, R. (2012). Online learning based on essential concepts and formative assessment. *Journal of Engineering Education, 101*(2), 244-287.

Le, H., Janssen, J., & Wubbels, T. (2018). Collaborative learning practices: Teacher and student perceived obstacles to effective student collaboration. *Cambridge Journal of Education, 48*(1), 103-122.

Leahy, W., & Sweller, J. (2008). The imagination effect increases with an increased intrinsic cognitive load. *Applied Cognitive Psychology: The Official Journal of the Society for Applied Research in Memory and Cognition, 22*(2), 273-283.

LEAP Innovations (2017). *LEAP learning framework for personalized learning.* Retrieved November 14, 2017, from: http://leaplearningframework.org/

Lefebvre, H. (1991). *Critique of everyday life: Foundations for a sociology of the everyday* (Vol. 2). London, UK: Verso Books.

Lim, C. P. (2004). Engaging learners in online learning environments. *TechTrends, 48*(4), 16.

Liu, E. Z., & Lee, C.Y. (2013). Using peer feedback to improve learning via online peer assessment. *The Turkish Online Journal of Educational Technology, 12*(1), 187-199.

Magno, C. (2010). The role of metacognitive skills in developing critical thinking. *Metacognition and Learning, 5(2),* 137-156.

Maki, P.L. (2002). Developing an assessment plan to learn about student learning. *The Journal of Academic Librarianship 28*(1-2), 8–13.

Margana, M., & Widyantoro, A. (2017). Developing English textbooks oriented to higher order thinking skills for students of vocational high schools in Yogyakarta. *Journal of Language Teaching and Research, 8*(1), 26–38. https://doi: 10.17507/jltr.0801.04.

Martindale, C. (1999). Biological bases of creativity. In R. J. Sternberg (Ed.), *Handbook of creativity* (pp. 137–152). Cambridge, UK: Cambridge University Press.

Marquis, E., & Vajoczki, S. (2012). Creative differences: Teaching creativity across the disciplines. *International Journal for the Scholarship of Teaching and Learning, 6*(1), 1-15.

Marzano, R. J. (2003). *What works in schools.* Alexandria, VA: ASCD.

Marzano, R. J., Pickering, D., & Pollock, J. E. (2001). *Classroom instruction that works: Research-based strategies for increasing student achievement.* Alexandria, VA: ASCD.

Mastergeorgeb, A., & Webba, N. (2003). Promoting effective helping behavior in peer-directed groups. *International Journal of Educational Research, 39,* 73-97.

Mayer, R. E., & Moreno, R. (2002). Aids to computer-based multimedia learning. *Learning and instruction, 12*(1), 107-119.

McCabe, A., & O'Connor, U. (2014). Student-centered learning: The role and responsibility of the lecturer. *Teaching in Higher Education, 19*(4) 350–359. https://doi.org/10.1080/13562517.2013.860111.

McCurdy, R. P., Nickels, M. L., & Bush, S. B. (2020). Problem-based design thinking tasks: Engaging student empathy in STEAM. *The Electronic Journal for Research in Science & Mathematics Education, 24*(2), 22-55.

Mehalik, M. M., Doppelt, Y., & Schuun, C. D. (2008). Middle-school science through design-based learning versus scripted inquiry: Better overall science concept learning and equity gap reduction. *Journal of Engineering Education, 97*(1), 71-85.

Memmert, D. (2007). Can creativity be improved by an attention-broadening training program? An exploratory study focusing on team sports. *Creativity Research Journal, 19*(2-3), 281-291.

Merriam-Webster. (2021). *Concept*. In https://www.merriam-webster.com. Retrieved February 20, 2021, from https://www.merriam-webster.com/dictionary/concept.

Michael (2006). Where's the evidence that active learning works? *Advances in Physiology Education, 4*(30), 159–67. https://doi.org/10.1152/advan.00053.2006.

Moeller, A. J., Theiler, J. M., & Wu, C. (2012). Goal setting and student achievement: A longitudinal study. *The Modern Language Journal, 96*(2), 153-169.

Molebash, P. E., Lee, J. K., & Heinecke, W. F. (2019). Teaching and learning inquiry framework. *Journal of Curriculum and Teaching, 8*(1), 20-31.

Mohd, Y. K., Nik, M. R. N. Y., Hamidah, Y. A., & Kamarul-Zaman, A. G. (2016). Inculcation of higher order thinking skills (hots) in Arabic language teaching at Malaysian primary schools. *Creative Education, 7*(2), 307-314. http://dx.doi.org/10.4236/ce.2016.72030

Moore, M. G., & Kearsley, G. (2011). *Distance education: A systems view of online learning*. Stamford, CT: Cengage Learning.

Moreno, R. (2004). Decreasing cognitive load for novice students: Effects of explanatory versus corrective feedback in discovery-based multimedia. *Instructional Science, 32*(1), 99-113.

Narciss, S., & Huth, K. (2004). *Instructional Design for Multimedia Learning,* 181195.

Nicol, D. J., & McFarlane-Dick, D. (2006). Formative assessment and self-regulated learning: A model and seven principles of good feedback practice. *Studies in Higher Education, 31,* 199–218.

Ng, K. C. (2007). Replacing face-to-face tutorials by synchronous online technologies: Challenges and pedagogical implications. *The International Review of Research in Open and Distance Learning, 8*(1) 1-15.

Oberg, C. (2010). Guiding classroom instruction through performance assessment. *Journal of Case Studies in Accreditation and Assessment, 1,* 1-11.

Orellana, P. (2010). Maieutic frame presence and quantity and quality of argumentation in Paideia seminar. Doctoral dissertation. University of North Carolina.

Packard, R. (2013). *Education transformation: How K-12 online learning is bringing the greatest change to education in 100 years.* Hillsboro, OR: Beyond Words.

Partnership for 21st-century skills. (2009a). *P21 framework definitions.* Retrieved from http://www.p21.org/documents/P21_Framework_Definitions.pdf

Partnership for 21st-century skills. (2009). *Learning for the 21st century: A report and mile guide for 21st-century skills.* ERIC Clearinghouse

Pak, M. (2015). Developing academic technology skills with WebQuests. *California English, 21*(1), 11-13. Retrieved from http://search.ebscohost.com/login.aspx?direct=true HYPERLINK

Pihlgren, A. S. (2008). Socrates in the classroom. Rationales and effects of philosophizing with children. Doctoral dissertation. Pedagogical institution, Stockholm University.

Pizzini, E.L., & Shepardson, D.P. (1991). Student questioning in the presence of the teacher during problem solving in science. *School Science and Mathematics, 91*(8), 348-352.

Puentedura, R. R. (2013). *SAMR: Getting to transformation.* Retrieved May 31, 2021.

Rauth, I., Köppen, E., Jobst, B., & Meinel, C. (2010). Design thinking: An educational model toward creative confidence. In *DS 66-2: Proceedings of the 1st international conference on design creativity (ICDC 2010).*

Rawle, F., Thuna, M., Zhao, T., & Kaler, M. (2018). Audio Feedback: Student and teaching assistant perspectives on an alternative mode of feedback for written assignments. *Canadian Journal for the Scholarship of Teaching and Learning, 9*(2), 2.

Reid, A., & Petocz, P. (2004). Learning domains and the process of creativity. *The Australian Educational Researcher 31*(2), 45-62.

Repetto, J., Cavanaugh, C., Wayer, N., & Liu, F. (2010). Virtual high schools: Improving outcomes for students with disabilities. *Quarterly Review of Distance Education, 11*(2), 91.

Rhoads, M. (2021). *Navigating the toggled term: A guide for K-12 classroom and school leaders.* Bern, Switzerland: Peter Lang US. Retrieved Mar 11, 2021, from https://www.peterlang. com/view/title/75300

Rogers, M. (2003). *Diffusion of innovations* (5th ed.). New York: Free Press.

Roschelle, J., & Teasley S.D. (1995) The construction of shared knowledge in collaborative problem solving. *In C.E. O'Malley (Ed), Computer-Supported Collaborative Learning.* (pp. 69-197). Berlin: Springer-Verlag

Rowe, P. G. (1987). *Design thinking*. Cambridge, MA: MIT Press.

Sam, P., & Rajan, P. (2013). Using graphic organizers to improve reading comprehension skills for middle school ESL students. *English Language Teaching, 6*(2), 155-170.

Scheer, A., Noweski, C., & Meinel, C. (2012). Transforming constructivist learning into action: Design thinking in education. *Design and Technology Education: An International Journal, 17*(3), 8-19.

Schneider, W. (2001). Metacognitive development: Educational implications. *International Encyclopedia of the Social and Behavioral Sciences*. pp. 9730-9733. Center for Advanced Study in the Behavioral Sciences, Stanford, CA.

Schneider, J. (2018). How genius hour helps kids connect what they're learning in school to their future goals - EdSurge news. EdSurge. Retrieved from https://www.edsurge.com/news/2018-09-19-how-genius-hour-helps-kids-connect-what-they-re-learning-in-school-to-their-future-goals.

Schwab, J.T. (1973). The Practical 3: Translation into curriculum. *The School Review, 81*(4): 501–522. DOI: https://doi.org/10.1080/00220272.2013.798838

Shute, V. J. (2008). Focus on formative feedback. *Review of educational research, 78*(1), 153-189.

Simon, H. A. (1969). *The sciences of the artificial*. Cambridge, MA: MIT Press.

Song, S. H., & Keller, J. M. (2001). Effectiveness of motivationally adaptive computer-assisted instruction on the dynamic aspects of motivation. *Educational Technology Research and Development, 49*(2), 5-22.

Stahl, G. (2000). A model of collaborative knowledge-building. In *Fourth international conference of the learning sciences* (Vol. 10, pp. 70-77). Mahwah, NJ: Erlbaum, 2000a.

Stephens, G. E., & Roberts, K. L. (2017). Facilitating collaboration in online groups. *Journal of Educators Online, 14*(1), 1-16.

Sternberg, R. J., & Lubart, T. I. (1999). The concept of creativity: Prospects and paradigms. In Sternberg Robert J (Ed.), *Handbook of Creativity* (pp. 3–15). New York, NY: Cambridge University Press.

Stassen, M., Doherty, K., & Poe, M. (2001). Program-based review and assessment: Tools and techniques for program improvement. Office of Academic Planning and Assessment (OAPA), University of Massachusetts, Amherst. Retrieved from http://www.umass.edu/oapa/oapa/publications/online_handbooks/program_based.pdf

Stetter, M. E., & Hughes, M. T. (2017). Using webquests to promote reading comprehension for students with learning disabilities. In *Society for Information Technology & Teacher Education International Conference* (pp. 2262-2268). Association for the Advancement of Computing in Education (AACE).

Sweller, J. (1988). Cognitive load during problem-solving: Effects on learning. *Cognitive Science, 12*, 257–285. https://doi.org/10.1207/s15516709cog1202_4.

Takeuchi, H., Taki, Y., Hashizume, H., Sassa, Y., Nagase, T., Nouchi, R., & Kawashima, R. (2011). Failing to deactivate: The association between brain activity during a working memory task and creativity. *NeuroImage, 55*(2), 681–687.

Tomlinson, C. A., & Imbeau, M. B. (2010). *Leading and managing a differentiated classroom.* Alexandria, VA: ASCD.

Tsai, K. C. (2013). A Review of the effectiveness of creative training on adult learners. *Journal of Social Science Studies, 1*(1), 17. https://doi.org/10.5296/jsss.v1i1.4329

Thomas, N. J. (2014). *Dual coding and common coding theories of memory.* Retrieved February 20, 2021, from https://plato.stanford.edu/entries/mental-imagery/theories-memory.html

Tobin, D. (2017). "Build your personal learning network," from https://www.linkedin.com/pulse/build-your-personal-learning-network-daniel-tobin/

Van Gog, T., Sluijsmans, D. M., Joosten-ten Brinke, D., & Prins, F. J. (2010). Formative assessment in an online learning environment to support flexible on-the-job learning in complex professional domains. *Educational Technology Research and Development*, *58*(3), 311-324.

Van Merriënboer, J. J. G. , Jelsma, O, & Paas, F. G. W. C. (1992). Training for reflective expertise: A four-component instructional design model for complex cognitive skills. *Educational Technology Research and Development, 40*(2), 23–43.

Vartanian, O. (2013). Fostering creativity: Insights from neuroscience. In O. Vartanian, A. S. Bristol, & J. C. Kaufman (Eds.), Neuroscience of creativity. Retrieved from http://public.eblib.com/choice/publicfullrecord. aspx? p=3339674

Wei, W., Dongsheng, L., & Chun, L. (2013). Fixed-wing aircraft interactive flight simulation and training STEAM based on XNA. In X. Zhang, Z. Zhou, Q. Wang & X. Luo (Eds.), *Proceedings of the 2013 International Conference on Virtual Reality and Visualization* (pp. 191-198). Xian, Shaanxi, China: IEEE.

Wenger, E., White, N., & Smith, D. (2009). *Digital Habitats: Stewarding technology for community.* Portland, OR: CP Square.

Wiliam, D. (2012). Feedback: Part of a system. *Educational Leadership, 70*(1), 31–34.

Willingham, D. T. (2009). *Why don't students like school?: A cognitive scientist answers questions about how the mind works and what it means for the classroom.* Hoboken, New Jersey: John Wiley & Sons.

Yahya, A. A., Toukal, Z., & Osman, A. (2012). Bloom's taxonomy-based classification for item bank questions using support vector machines. *In Modern Advances in Intelligent Systems and Tools* (pp. 135-140). Berlin, Germany: Springer.

Yang, C., Luo, L., Vadillo, M. A., Yu, R., & Shanks, D. R. (2021). Testing (quizzing) boosts classroom learning: A systematic and meta-analytic review. *Psychological Bulletin, 147*(4), 399.

Yenmez, A. A., Özpinar, İ., & Gökçe, S. (2017). Use of webquests in mathematics instruction: Academic achievement, teacher and student opinions. *Universal Journal of Educational Research, 5*(9), 1554-1570.

Zainuddin, H. & Moore, R. A. (2003). Enhancing Critical thinking with structured controversial dialogues. *The Internet TESL Journa*l, 9(6), 1-56.

Zeiser, K., Scholz, C., & Cirks, V. (2018). Maximizing student agency: Implementing and measuring student-centered learning practices. *American Institutes for Research, 1*, 1-59.

Zimmerman, B. J., Bandura, A., & Martinez-Pons, M. (1992). Self-motivation for academic attainment: The role of self-efficacy beliefs and personal goal setting. *American Educational Research Journal, 29*(3), 663-676.

Zion, M., Michalsky, T., & Mevarech, Z. R. (2005). The effects of metacognitive instruction embedded within an asynchronous learning network on scientific inquiry skills. *International Journal of Science Education, 27*(8), 957-983.

Zohar, A., Weinberger, Y., & Tamir, P. (1994). The effect of the biology critical thinking project on the development of critical thinking. *Journal of Research in Science Teaching, 31*(2), 183-196.

LIST OF FIGURES

LIST OF TABLES

ABOUT THE AUTHORS

Matthew Rhoads, Ed.D. is an expert and innovator in educational technology and instructional strategy integration within online, blended, and traditional in-person classroom settings. As a practicing educator in K-12, Adult Education, and higher education, he develops EdTech tool integrations with instructional strategies to drive instruction. He also has expertise in instructing teachers and educational leaders on how to utilize data to make data-driven decisions to drive instruction as well as has developed a data literacy curriculum for K-12 educators. Dr. Rhoads publications focus on instructional and organizational frameworks that help K-12 schools toggle between various educational settings and integrating research-based instructional strategies with mainstream EdTech tools to amplify student learning within any classroom setting. His latest books include *Navigating the Toggled Term: A Guide for K-12 Classroom and School Leaders* and the *Amplify Learning: A Global Collaborative series*. He also has his podcast, Navigating Education - The Podcast, which discusses all topics related to education, instruction, policy, and coaching. For more information on Dr. Rhoads and his work, visit his website at www.matthewrhoads.com. You can connect with him on Twitter @mattrhoads1990.

Shannon Moore is a Teacher on Special Assignment (TOSA) for the Educator Support department in her district. She values connections, communication, innovation, creativity, and progressive-thinking in the classroom. She believes in educational transformation through the use of best practices supplemented by diverse EdTech tools. As a Google for Education Certified Trainer, she aims to enhance the practices of educators everywhere by providing relevant and thoughtful approaches to instructional design and delivery and supporting them in the implementation process. Additionally, she is a firm believer in the power that rests in integrating creativity into every facet of classroom practice and as an Adobe Education Leader commits to ensuring students are given the chance to creatively exemplify their understanding and educators feel confident in taking creative risks to maximize student learning. When she is not working on changing the world of education, she is hanging out with her husband and her two cats, or reading a good book while sipping a hot cup of coffee. Connect with her on Twitter: @Smoore_Teach

Janelle Clevenger McLaughlin is an Education Consultant for Advanced Learning Partnerships working with districts all across the United States. She is a former curriculum director for Manchester Community Schools in Indiana where she led the high ability and RTI programming, curriculum development, 1:1 implementation, and professional development initiatives. Prior to that role, Ms. McLaughlin spent 14 years as a classroom teacher. Her experiences as a consultant range from job-embedded coaching for teachers and administrators, to leading reflective collaborations and facilitating action-plan development. She has a strong belief in the power of education and the role leaders play in building a strong foundation for the organization. She has worked with educational leaders in over thirty different states and two countries. She has presented on numerous topics at national and international events. Her latest book, *Leadership at Every Level: Five Qualities of Effective Classroom, School, and District Leaders* is available through Solution Tree and Amazon. Her greatest joys come from laughing with her two teens, Sydney and Evan. Connect with her on social media linked on her website: www.innovativeeducationsolutions.net.

EduMatch

PUBLISHING